the
hardest
help

the
hardest
help

Supporting a Loved One
Through Alcoholism

HOLLY THORTON

HCT Publishing
HCT Press

The Hardest Help
Supporting a Loved One Through Alcoholism

COPYRIGHT © 2025 Holly Thorton
Published by HCT Publishing, a division of HCT Press

Published by HCT Publishing, a division of HCT Press

HCT Publishing
HCT Press

eBook ISBN: 979-8-9987577-0-9
Paperback ISBN: 979-8-9987577-1-6
Hardcover ISBN: 979-8-9987577-2-3
Library of Congress Control Number: 2025909700

First Edition
Book Production and Publishing by Brands Through Books
brandsthroughbooks.com

TheHardestHelp.com

Privacy Statement

While the clients' stories shared in this book are true, names and some details have been changed to protect their privacy.

This publication contains the opinions and ideas of its author. It is intended to provide helpful and informative material on the subjects addressed. The strategies outlined in this book may not be suitable for every individual and are not guaranteed or warranted to provide any particular results.

This book is sold with the understanding that neither the author nor the publisher is engaged in rendering legal, financial, accounting, or other professional advice or services. The reader should consult a competent professional before adopting any of the suggestions in this book or drawing inferences from it.

No warranty is made with respect to the accuracy or completeness of the information or references contained herein, and both the authors and the publisher specifically disclaim any responsibility for any liability, loss, or risk, personal or otherwise, that is incurred as a consequence, directly or indirectly, of the use and application of any of the contents of this book.

Table of Contents

Foreword

This is the book for anyone who has discovered a loved one's substance use and is living in fear of what to do. For the wife who has questioned her own sanity over their partner's drinking. For the mother who waits up at night, unable to sleep, wondering where their child is and whether they are alive. For the sibling who yells out in anger—"why can't you just stop"—debating whether to cut them off or give them one more chance. Holly's words offer family members the support and knowing they crave—honesty without blame, vulnerability without victimhood, and an unwavering drive to turn pain into purpose.

As someone who works closely with families impacted by addiction, I've witnessed how isolating and overwhelming it can be to love someone who is actively struggling. So many books either speak to the addict, or speak at the family. This book speaks *with* them. *The Hardest Help* is the book I wish more people had when they first walk into my office—raw, real, and rooted in hope.

Holly doesn't offer empty promises or clinical jargon. What she offers is lived experience, powerful storytelling, and practical tools that meet people where they are. Her journey through grief, chaos, and healing is not only relatable—it's instructive. What makes this book especially valuable is how she combines her personal experience with actionable tools from the CRAFT method—a model I teach every day to families navigating addiction.

You'll find no shame here. No quick fixes. Just a compassionate, empowering roadmap for anyone trying to support a loved one through alcoholism without losing themselves in the process.

If you've picked up this book, you're likely searching for clarity, answers, or maybe just someone who understands what you're going through. You've found that here. Families all over the world have used the very same tools Holly offers to help improve relationships with their loved ones and positively encourage them into treatment. Holly's story is a lifeline—and a reminder that even in the darkest moments, there is still a way forward.

Michelle Kuecker, LCSW, LAC
CRAFT Trainer and Substance Use Counselor
Robert J. Meyers, PhD and Associates

Introduction

His breathing was labored, each gasp desperate and strained. His body fought for every breath, his chest rising and falling in a frantic rhythm. I could see it, hear it—the struggle, the suffering. Panic gripped me as I stood frozen, helpless. I couldn't fix this. I couldn't save him.

I rushed into the nurses' station, screaming, crying, begging them to do something. "Please! CPR! Please!" I couldn't watch him suffer. The medical team sprang into action, the sharp sound of chest compressions echoing through the air. In the corner of the room, our son stood sobbing uncontrollably, witnessing the unthinkable—something no teenager should ever have to see.

I never imagined that meeting the man who I thought was the love of my life would become a cautionary tale, let alone living the nightmare that followed. How did we go from being so in love, so happy, to watching Steve slip away because of alcohol? Looking back, it feels surreal.

Back then, I thought our biggest fight would be about whether we were watching a sleazy reality show or one of his action-packed movies. I never imagined we'd be facing down liver failure.

Steve was everything I ever wanted. He was hilarious, turned negatives into positives, and had a charm that could light up any room. If you ask anyone who knew him what they remember most, they'd say, "He was so funny." He was always making people laugh, and he definitely made me laugh. He was handsome, with dark hair, hazel eyes, and a confident, adventurous spirit. I'd known him since I was thirteen, watching him grow from a carefree teen into a hardworking, entrepreneurial man who could cook, rebuild engines, and find joy in every adventure.

Have you ever met someone who instantly felt like home? That's how I felt with Steve. After reconnecting later in life, I knew we'd be inseparable. We wanted the same things: a home, a family, a simple, happy life.

One of the reasons I chose Steve was that he made me feel safe. When I was with him, it felt like everything was right in the world, and nothing external could shake that. He had this take-charge attitude that put me at ease. I felt like as long as I followed his lead, everything would work out because he had it handled. I trusted him completely.

Steve was also incredibly honest—sometimes a little too honest. I knew if I asked his opinion, he'd tell me exactly what he thought, for better or worse. But what mattered most was how emotionally vulnerable he was with me. He wasn't afraid to express his feelings, to look me in the eye and tell me how important I was to him and how deeply committed he was to our life together. When he looked at me that way—piercing my soul and seducing me with his words—I melted every time.

We had so much fun together. Both of us had a spontaneous spirit, and it wasn't unusual for us to wake up one morning and decide to do something adventurous, like driving to the mountains to go sledding or heading off on a road trip without a plan, just to see where we'd end up. We started a family, but we never lost that spontaneous spirit.

I'll never forget one of those last-minute decisions, when we decided to go on a weekend getaway to the Oregon coast on one of the busiest days of the year.

We quickly packed a bag, put the kids in the car, and hit the road. Along the way, we stopped for lunch, visited the aquarium, got ice cream, and spent hours playing on the beach. By the time we were ready to rest, we rolled into the nearest hotel, only to find out the entire town was completely booked. Undeterred, we drove to the next town, hoping to find a room, but that town was booked, too. By 11 p.m., our only option was to turn around and drive the three hours back home. Even though it wasn't what we planned, we laughed about it the whole way home. That was just who we were together—spontaneous and willing to turn even a setback into an adventure.

I loved that about him. He knew I needed that spontaneity, and he brought that out in me often. It wasn't just the big things, like spontaneous trips. He could be just as spontaneous with gifts, both big and small. He'd surprise me with a new pair of earrings or find a beautiful flower in the yard and give it to me, just because. He knew me like the back of his hand, and those little gestures mattered so much.

When I surprised Steve with the news of our first pregnancy, his joy was palpable. He set up the nursery the next day. At that moment, life really did feel perfect.

In those first few years of marriage, alcohol was often part of our outings, but it didn't seem excessive. I grew up in a family that didn't drink, so I brushed it off as normal because that's what he told me was normal, and I didn't have anything to compare it to. I was told it was just something young couples do. Steve balanced everything so beautifully—work, family, and making me feel loved and cared for.

Over the next few years, we had more children, and life was good. He was a great dad. He was the fun one who got down on the floor to play with the kids and their toys. He handled most of the cooking, never missed an activity, and still managed to prioritize our relationship. Whether it was date nights, surprise gifts, or making my favorite meals, he made a point to show how much he cared. For years, I felt like things in our home were ideal.

But subtle signs of trouble began to emerge. Of course, these things start small—discoveries around the house, like liquor disguised in a drinking glass we would typically only serve water in. Steve started drinking more and more. I found a hidden gallon of vodka. When I brought it up, he dismissed my concerns, assuring me everything was fine. I wanted to believe him, so I did.

To this day, people ask me, "How could you not know what was going on?" At the time, it didn't feel obvious. Things didn't fall apart overnight; it was gradual.

The best answer I can give is that I trusted him. When you've lived with someone for years and built that trust, it's easy to dismiss small changes. Things don't go from ideal to terrible overnight. The shift is subtle, and by the time you realize it, so much damage has already been done.

Looking back now, I can see how much my kids were suffering, too, though it wasn't always obvious at the time. Kids are resilient. They could be fearful one moment during one of Steve's emotional episodes and loving toward him the next. They craved that normalcy, that acceptance and affection from their dad. But over time, I could see they were wearing down. They had silently endured the emotional roller coaster our lives had become.

There's a silent emotional struggle that happens when you live with this kind of chaos. You want it to end, and after a while, you don't care how it ends—even if it means the person doesn't survive. That sounds terrible to say, and I've carried so much guilt over that feeling.

There was this push and pull going on emotionally. I'd cry, begging God to just rip the Band-Aid off. I'd pray, "If this is how it's going to end, then let it end now and take him with you." That's how emotionally intense and tormenting the situation was—for me and for my kids.

Whether it was another hospital stay, sitting on edge wondering if Steve would survive, or another fight over alcohol, we were exhausted. I don't think my kids could articulate it then, but I know now that's what we all felt. And they're still dealing with that guilt today.

After our third child, Steve gradually changed. He became distant, short-tempered, and restless. On Valentine's weekend, he drank excessively at a resort, leading to a public argument and our removal from the property. I was embarrassed, and for the first time, I began to seriously question whether his drinking was escalating.

A week later, he called me at work saying he didn't feel well. A rash and back pain turned out to be kidney failure from heavy drinking. He was rushed to the hospital. Steve downplayed the severity, and I believed him, trusting it was a one-time issue. I took him home after forty-eight hours, not realizing it was the start of something far worse.

A month later, Steve admitted he needed help and entered a detox program. I was hopeful, but just days after I picked him up, he ordered a beer at dinner. He assured me he had it under control. I tried to believe him, but a sinking feeling had already taken hold.

Over time, Steve's drinking escalated. Confrontations made him defensive, and he began blaming me, saying my stress caused him to drink. His out-of-character comments—like calling us a "ball and chain"—felt like he was pushing us away.

By New Year's Eve, he was drinking heavily, celebrating at home. The next day, Steve came home devastated. A co-worker had reported him for drinking on the job, and he lost his position after a blood alcohol test confirmed he was over the legal limit.

That loss devastated him. He now felt emasculated and without purpose. He became even more withdrawn, slipping further away from the man he once was. The weight of that failure hit hard, and I could see the hopelessness setting in. I was watching him give up, surrendering to the bottle.

For a long time, I believed that Steve's drinking was occasional, something manageable. Over time, I realized it had become more regular, but I still didn't see it as something I needed to monitor. What I didn't know was that he had been drinking at home all along—not to get drunk, but just enough to maintain his daily life, complete his tasks as a husband and father, and avoid withdrawals.

Even then, I didn't recognize it as truly excessive—not until much later, just weeks before he went into the hospital. I never could have imagined it would become something that could completely take over someone's life.

The man who once had boundless drive now seemed aimless, drinking a half gallon of vodka daily. I tried to maintain a sense of normalcy with family outings and date nights, but his health was rapidly declining.

On what would be our last normal weekend, we went to the beach and returned home, but Steve wasn't well. Each day, he grew weaker, sleeping sixteen hours, eating less, drinking less, and struggling to breathe. His skin turned yellow, and he was too weak to move without help.

Watching him physically deteriorate was terrifying. So was the unknown. But somehow, I kept telling myself it would get better.

Until one day, I couldn't keep up the narrative anymore. And surprisingly, Steve agreed that he needed medical attention.

I rushed him to the hospital, where he was admitted to the ICU. Dr. Wanek bluntly told me to pull my head out of the sand: Steve was in full liver and multi-organ failure.

He was placed in a medically induced coma, and doctors warned me his survival was unlikely. In my mind, when my world flipped upside down, it truly felt like the rug had been pulled out from under me. It was a shock.

I had to start processing what had happened, and my reaction surprised the medical team, friends, and family. They had a hard time understanding why I was so blindsided. But you have to understand: I only allowed myself to see what he told me and wanted me to see.

The ICU became my second home, and the stress broke me. I needed sedatives just to endure it.

Miraculously, Steve recovered after three months in the ICU. After several harrowing months, he was discharged and came home. I staged an intervention with his father and brother, urging him into treatment at Betty Ford. He reluctantly agreed, and for a while, there was progress. But anxiety took over, and he left treatment prematurely, despite warnings from the staff. Within days, Steve resumed drinking, and my hope dwindled.

In the months that followed, hospitalizations became frequent—every six weeks or so. I was drowning in anxiety, juggling work, parenting, and watching Steve destroy himself. I finally reached my breaking point. I told him I wouldn't be talked into going to the liquor store for him anymore. I poured out his alcohol, diluted bottles with water, and hid them in places he couldn't reach. But Steve retaliated. He slashed my tires, smashed dishes, and burned my clothes. It felt like a demon had taken over.

At the time, I didn't fully understand what was happening. Steve's anger and erratic behavior came from a mix of emotional and physical factors. He felt angry, emasculated, and out of control. But it wasn't just emotional—it was physical. His liver and kidneys were failing, and the toxins his body could no longer filter were starting to affect his brain. Hepatic encephalopathy—a condition caused by high ammonia levels—was changing him into someone I didn't recognize. While this explanation doesn't excuse his behavior, it helped me understand why his actions became so unpredictable and frightening.

My kids were deeply affected by what our home had become. They never knew if they'd come back to a calm evening or a nightmare. Two incidents stand out vividly, and I know they will stay with my children forever.

The first happened one morning when I left to go grocery shopping with the younger kids. My oldest daughter, who was eight at the time, stayed home to play at a friend's house next door. She came home before I did and was in the house with him when he sliced his leg. She watched him bleed all over the couch. About ten minutes before I got home, I received a text from Steve: "You'd better hurry." I assumed it was just him being bored or needy, as usual.

When we arrived, we began bringing in the groceries. I could see Steve sitting on the couch, smiling at me like everything was fine. But within moments, I heard the kids screaming. I ran into the living room to find Steve sitting there, blood pouring from a deep cut on his leg. A knife lay beside him.

The house descended into chaos. The kids were crying and terrified, and I was trying to calm them down while figuring out what to do. I knew Steve needed medical attention. I told my son not to call 911, thinking I could take Steve to urgent care myself. But before I could stop him, he'd already made the call.

Minutes later, the police and paramedics arrived. As they treated his leg, Steve told them that I had done this to him. Hearing their father accuse me of hurting him was devastating for the kids. They knew it wasn't true, but seeing Steve behave this way was terrifying and confusing for them. That moment is burned into my memory as one of the many times I felt helpless against what was happening to my family.

Not long after that incident, the second—even more haunting—happened in our driveway. Steve had been pacing all day, having an emotional meltdown, when he suddenly went into the truck with his gun. My son, who was fourteen at the time, immediately understood what was happening. He ran after Steve, climbed into the truck, and wrestled him for the gun.

As they struggled, the gun went off. The shot hit the wood paneling above the garage. My son came back into the house trembling, crying, and utterly exhausted. Not just from that moment but from the weight of everything he had been carrying. The constant fear for Steve, for our safety, for his family.

That moment broke something in all of us. I realized how close we were to losing not only Steve but the safety and stability of our entire family.

You'd think that would have been the final straw, but it wasn't. That came a few days later.

I woke early one morning to find Steve leaning over me, his hands tangled in my hair, pulling it. He was muttering in a low, chilling voice. Gibberish. His tone sent a shiver down my spine. My heart raced as I lay frozen, silently praying he would come to his senses and not harm me. At that moment, I knew Steve was just a shell of himself. He needed more help than I could give. If something didn't change, my life was in jeopardy.

The next day, I went to the courthouse and obtained a restraining order. By that evening, Steve had been escorted from our home.

For the first time in years, I felt safe. I began researching how to help him and discovered the CRAFT method— Community Reinforcement and Family Training. It focuses on encouraging positive change, improving communication, and increasing the likelihood of treatment, all while teaching families to care for themselves. I started implementing these techniques. While Steve didn't stop drinking, our communication improved. He even began talking about long-term treatment.

After months of living at his parents' home and slowly rebuilding communication, Steve called to say he wasn't feeling well. The moment he described his symptoms, I knew. My medical background told me exactly what he was facing: the end stage of liver failure. I brought him to the hospital, where the ICU doctor confirmed my fears. I called his family to come say their goodbyes.

Steve and I spent his final moments talking about everything but his illness—our favorite show, our favorite foods. We talked as if nothing was wrong. Part of that was because he didn't fully understand the seriousness of his condition, and that's exactly how I wanted it.

I wanted our last moments to be calm. I wanted us to feel connected, free of any anxiety that might taint those memories.

I focused on his voice, his smile, and the feeling of holding his hand, committing it all to memory. As his ammonia levels rose, he slipped into a coma and passed away within twenty-four hours.

At that point, I remained relatively calm. Looking back, I knew logically what was happening. I understood medically that we had hours together, not days, but my heart hadn't accepted it yet. I was able to stay calm and present for him, and I'm so grateful I could.

I stayed by his side until late that night, then went back home to get some rest. Early the next morning, I woke to a call urging me to hurry back—his breathing had become labored.

When I arrived, Steve was in immense distress, struggling for every breath, each one taking all the strength he had left. The composure I'd had the night before was gone. I burst into tears and collapsed to the floor. At that moment, I felt like my life was ending too.

The weight of his suffering was unbearable. It was as if I could feel his labored breathing, and I didn't think I could go on watching him like that.

I ran to the doctor, begging for Steve to be placed on a ventilator to end his suffering more peacefully. Afterward, I returned to his bedside, took his hand once again, and tried to memorize every detail—what his fingers felt like intertwined with mine, the warmth of his touch.

We rested like that for the next few hours while family members came in to say their goodbyes.

I didn't write this book because I wanted to. I wrote it because I had to—so no one else would feel as alone, unprepared, and heartbroken as I did.

This was not a happy ending. It's a gut-wrenching cautionary tale, but it isn't the end of the story. Through it all, I learned the hard way and gained lessons I wish I had known much earlier. In the chapters ahead, I'll share what I discovered, what I would have done differently knowing what I know now, and how you can use these lessons to change the course for yourself and your loved one.

If you're here searching for hope, you're not alone. You don't have to stay stuck in fear and heartbreak. Throughout this book, you'll learn to recognize what alcoholism really looks like, how to spot the red flags, how to respond in ways that encourage change, and how to guide your loved one toward recovery. I'll show you a practical path that gives you the best possible chance at a better outcome while also protecting your own mental health along the way.

Chapter 1 is where our journey together begins, so let's dive in.

CHAPTER 1

The Beginning of Everything

It wasn't until alcohol ripped everything from my life that I finally opened my eyes to the truth about Steve. Alcohol had never been part of my life, but somehow, it became the center of my world.

Growing up, alcohol was non-existent. If my parents or family members drank, they did so privately or only on social occasions. I never saw a bottle of liquor or a beer in the house. I didn't view alcohol as good or bad. It just wasn't something I had an opinion about because it didn't exist in my day-to-day life.

My parents were very health-conscious. Not only did I grow up without alcohol, but I didn't even have soda or sugar. I was the weird kid at the lunch table with the brown bread when everyone else had white bread, a carrot when everyone else had Fruit Roll-Ups, and maybe some SunChips while the cool kids had Mr. Squeeze drinks—if you're old enough to remember those. My diet was full of whole foods and organic options. Basically, if it wasn't sprouted or grown locally, it didn't make it into the house.

That sheltered, health-focused upbringing shaped how I would one day envision a family of my own—one free from the chaos I would come to know. I pictured raising my kids in a calm, stable environment, just like the one I had. Looking back now, it's so ironic how different their childhood turned out from what I had imagined—shaped by circumstances I never could have predicted.

As I got older, I realized many adults enjoy drinking. I saw people go out for drinks after work and drinking in restaurants, and I learned about "mom wine culture." But it never dawned on me to start drinking—because it just wasn't part of my routine.

Sure, I tried it a few times, but I didn't like the taste or how it made me feel. I decided alcohol just wasn't for me. It just never became part of my life. Honestly, I thought skipping dinner and eating a box of chocolates was as wild as I'd ever get.

I've always believed we all have our preferences—like I love sushi, but not everyone does. I wanted to be accepting and let every adult make their own choices, so I never thought twice about anyone else's drinking habits.

When I pictured an alcoholic, I saw my great-uncle slumped over a barstool with a drink in his frail hand and a look of despair. I never imagined that my well-put-together husband would fit that mold. It took me a long time to understand what alcoholism truly is and to accept that Steve was an alcoholic.

Because I didn't grow up around alcohol and wasn't a drinker myself, spotting the signs was especially difficult. Like many people, I had a mental image of what an alcoholic looked and acted like. And if someone didn't fit that image, it was hard to recognize the problem.

Alcoholism can often be invisible to the naked eye. Only when you look closely—paying attention to subtle signs— does it begin to reveal itself.

Now, close your eyes and ask yourself: What does an alcoholic look like? How do they behave? Do they have a job? Are they successful? Are they respected in the community? Picture it for a moment.

These people are walking among us. Often, they appear to have it all together in the outside world. But when they go home, their drinking is out of control, affecting their health and relationships. And even if it hasn't bled into every aspect of their lives yet, the truth is that it will. It's only a matter of time.

The image of alcoholism in my mind looked exactly like this:

My uncle was very thin, malnourished from years of prioritizing hard liquor over food. He was disheveled, always wearing baggy, grungy clothes—a worn T-shirt and pants with holes in them. Growing up, we visited him once a year, and he passed away when I was sixteen. Out of all those visits, what stands out most is how we always found him at the corner bar. He lived in a small town, and if he wasn't at home, that's where we'd look. Sure enough, he'd be there, slumped in a corner. That bar was his second home, a daily habit that consumed him after losing his wife to cancer. He drowned his grief in alcohol and never recovered. His words were slurred, and he never seemed fully present. That was the alcoholic I envisioned.

But Steve? Steve didn't fit that mold at all.

Steve was present, full of life, and well put together. He cared about his appearance, loved a button-up shirt, and always wore his favorite cologne, giving him his signature scent. He wasn't physically fit in a gym-going sense, but his demanding job and constant home projects left him with muscular legs and toned arms. Steve was handsome, confident, and smelled like he had just stepped out of a magazine ad.

For years, I never saw Steve drunk. He was a great husband. He went to work, came home right after, and never once disappeared to a bar or a friend's house for drinks. He was present with me and the kids every single day.

He wasn't belligerent or slurring. He seemed completely coherent—the dad outside chatting with neighbors while the kids played in the yard. His charm masked a growing dependency none of us saw coming.

You see, alcoholism can be invisible, especially when someone knows how to mask it. Unless someone is visibly drunk or exhibiting concerning behaviors, it's easy to miss the signs, even when heavy drinking is happening. The contrast between Steve's outward appearance and his struggles behind closed doors made me realize how little I truly understood alcoholism.

To make sense of his drinking, I had to step back and ask, "What really is alcoholism?"

Have you ever wondered why one person can drink socially without consequence while another spirals into the depths of a disease?

The latter is exactly what Steve did for so long.

Reflecting back, my trust in Steve also shaped how I approached the delicate situation with our kids. When they asked about their dad's behavior, I'd downplay their questions and concerns, reassuring them that everything was fine.

I realize now that, in my efforts to protect them, I may have unintentionally blinded them to truths they needed to understand. I thought I was shielding them, but I can see now that it may have left them confused, angry, and struggling to make sense of what they saw and felt on their own.

Alcoholism doesn't always look like the stereotype you might picture. It doesn't always come with slurred words, disappearing acts, frequent bar visits, or alarming behavior.

Sometimes, alcoholism looks like cuddling up on the couch for a movie after dinner. It looks like a warm meal on the table when you come home. It looks like being greeted with a smile and a gentle hug after a long day.

I believe an alcoholic is not defined by their drinking. They didn't set out to become an alcoholic. It's just that their taste for alcohol turned into a frequency they couldn't control, and eventually, it spiraled into a disease—much like overeating can spiral into obesity.

Your loved one still wants to be the person you love. They still want to spend time with you, crack jokes, and be there for you emotionally. Even at my lowest point with Steve, I could still look at him without anger and share a tender moment. But that didn't mean that damage wasn't real or that boundaries weren't needed.

So, it left me wondering, as you might be wondering now, What is alcoholism?

It's a disease that lurks in the shadows behind routine and good intentions. And if you're not watching closely, it takes over.

It's important not only to understand what alcoholism is and why it develops but also to grasp the emotional toll it takes on your loved one.

Does it impact you emotionally? Absolutely. But your loved one is tormented daily by the obsession of when they'll have their next drink. If alcohol isn't in their hand, they're thinking about when they get off work so they can drink—or when you'll leave the room so they can sneak another sip.

There's also a lot of guilt and shame that comes with alcohol use disorder. There's a quiet war playing out in their mind every day. Alcohol has such a powerful pull, and your loved one doesn't want to disappoint you—or themselves— so there's this internal struggle. The drinking itself can bring shame—shame about how much they've consumed or how they behaved under the influence.

Alcoholism, or Alcohol Use Disorder (AUD), is a chronic condition where a person struggles to manage their drinking, even when it begins to harm their health, relationships, job, or daily life.[1]

It's not defined by how much a person drinks but by how their drinking affects them and those around them. Alcoholism exists on a broad spectrum, and it can take many forms.

For example, my mother-in-law is an alcoholic, but you won't catch her drunk. Instead, it shows up in her daily routine. Like clockwork, she's in front of the fridge at 4:00 p.m., cracking open a beer. She has four or five every night, day after day. She depends on it.

Others experience more severe forms of the disease, fitting the stereotype of slurred words, irritability, and impaired decision-making when under the influence.

Unlike social drinkers, who can control when and how much they consume, alcoholics develop a physical and psychological dependency. Without alcohol, their bodies may respond with symptoms like jitters, irritability, shakiness, or, in severe cases, seizures and even death from withdrawal. This dependency makes quitting difficult and, in many cases, dangerous without professional help.[2]

Over time, a person's tolerance increases. For example, someone who starts with a pint a day may eventually require a half gallon to achieve the same effect.

This escalating cycle places immense strain on the body, leading to serious health issues and complications at work, in relationships, and beyond. Left untreated, alcoholism can ruin lives, and it can be deadly.

When you discover your loved one is an alcoholic, it's normal to ask yourself why. There are so many factors at play, and it's important to remember that your loved one didn't wake up one day and decide to become an alcoholic. It's a combination of influences that create this storm. Genetics, psychology, environment, and societal norms all play a role in the development of this disease.

Genetics can predispose someone to alcoholism. A family history of the disease increases the likelihood that, if someone begins drinking, they may become dependent on alcohol.[3] This doesn't mean it's inevitable, but it creates a vulnerability.

Environment also plays a powerful role. Society has normalized daily drinking, encouraging us to order cocktails at dinner, raise a glass at celebrations, or unwind at workplace happy hours. It's easy to begin drinking in social settings. But for someone with a genetic predisposition, what starts as casual drinking can gradually develop into a more serious problem.

Psychological factors are equally significant. Many people turn to alcohol as a way to cope, much like others might use food or shopping to manage stress. For some, drinking provides temporary relief from emotional pain, anxiety, or trauma. Over time, though, this coping mechanism becomes a dependency.

For many, it's not just one factor but a combination of influences. Genetic vulnerability, societal normalization, psychological coping mechanisms, and environmental pressures all contribute to the perfect storm.

Alcoholism is complex, and there's no single thing that leads to it. That complexity is exactly why, if you want to address the disease effectively, you have to first take time to understand it from all angles.

According to health data, about one in thirteen adults admit to having an alcohol problem—but honestly, once you've lived through it, that number feels low. You start to notice how many people are silently struggling behind closed doors.[4]

But when you compare those numbers to what we know about early intervention and recovery, the difference is astounding.[5]

Studies consistently show that individuals who receive treatment earlier in the progression of their addiction have a much higher chance of long-term recovery.

Early intervention reduces the risk of serious consequences like DUI charges, accidents, irreversible health damage, or even death. It also helps prevent the addiction from becoming so deeply ingrained that it's harder to treat.[6]

These findings make one thing clear: Taking early action changes everything.

While it can be hard to recognize addiction—especially when your loved one is in denial—the earlier it's addressed, the better the odds for healing and recovery.

The numbers might be shocking, but early intervention offers real hope.

Recovery is possible, and when action is taken early, the road to that recovery is much more manageable.

But identifying this illness isn't always easy, especially when the person you love is doing everything they can to convince you there's no problem.

As I dove headfirst into the research, I realized just how many families are touched by this disease. You're not alone.

The research opened my eyes to how widespread alcoholism truly is, and I thought about all the families silently searching for hope. It wasn't until I began writing this book that I fully grasped the scale of the problem. These statistics are staggering, but when you're living through it, statistics are the last thing on your mind.

At the time, I felt so alone. I remember wondering if there were others out there who felt the same way—who were just as scared, confused, and desperate for answers.

I've now met so many families who were able to heal and recover, and that's why early detection matters so much. It truly can make all the difference.

In my case with Steve, I didn't understand at first how destructive alcohol already was in our lives. I kept waiting for him to be ready, trusting that he would recognize the issue on his own.

But the signs were there—glaringly obvious—long before he ever admitted anything.

I also didn't realize that the problem wasn't just the drinking—it was the ripple effects that would reshape our family and chip away at the life we'd built together.

For years, Steve was still the man I married: an engaged, loving father who helped with dinner, pitched in around the house, and showed up for us.

But beneath the surface, the disease was spreading like cancer. What I didn't consciously recognize then was how deeply Steve's drinking was already affecting the kids, even if they never said it out loud.

They saw the tension, felt the shifts in mood, and noticed the quiet arguments I tried to hide.

I can see now how hard they worked to keep the peace—how they tiptoed around their dad when they sensed he wasn't in a good place. They wanted to protect him, just like I did.

As tolerance for alcohol builds, more is required to feel normal, and this is where the real danger lies.

What started as a few beers to take the edge off became a pint of vodka just to calm his nerves. And over time, the cycle of consumption continued—more alcohol, more frequently—but still hidden behind daily life.

It wasn't just Steve's tolerance for alcohol that was growing. Everyone in our household was slowly adapting to what was our new normal without even realizing it.

The kids and I began to adjust our routines in order to accommodate changing behavior. The kids learned when to keep quiet, when to hide, and when it was okay to seek Steve's attention.

The most deceptive part of this progression is how gradual it can be.

The signs aren't always obvious at first, and in many cases, the changes are so slow that they almost go unnoticed. In my case, I adjusted to each new level of drinking without question.

As Steve's drinking increased, I didn't see the problem because he was still the person I loved. I wanted to believe everything was fine, even though I could feel that something wasn't.

You might find yourself in a similar position, where these changes happen so slowly that it's hard to figure out when things began to change.

It's easy to ignore all the signs because you're caught up in daily life, work, and kids. But by the time you realize that alcohol has become a problem, it's already an uphill battle.

Reflection Journal
Take a moment to reflect:

- When you picture alcoholism, what does it look like?

- Has that image changed after reading this chapter?

- Are there potential red flags you may have overlooked?

- Have you ever rationalized your loved one's behavior because they seem so high-functioning or "normal"?

Write your answers down. It will be powerful to look back on these reflections at the end of the book.

Take your time with these questions. Your reflections are an important part of understanding what you've lived through—and where you want to go.

CHAPTER 2

When the Seams Start to Show

It starts so quietly—just a few late nights and a drink to relax. But then it's every night. The bottles are no longer just on the counter—they're hidden. Conversations turn into slurred arguments. Promises are made, then broken. And you find yourself wondering, When did this become a problem? How did I end up constantly guessing what I'll find next?

If you're starting to notice changes in your loved one's behavior or daily routines, you might find yourself asking, When does drinking become a problem? Is it when they acknowledge it? Or when you feel it? If you're waiting for them to come to you and admit there's a problem, you might be waiting a long time.

Steve actually did come to me at one point and confess that he had a problem, but later recanted that admission once he realized he wasn't ready to put in the work it would take to get better.

Once he made that decision, the narrative changed. I was told over and over again that there wasn't a problem. I started to question myself because I didn't have anyone else to confirm my feelings—and the one other person in the room, my husband, was adamant there was no issue. If you hear something enough, you can start to believe it.

Looking back, I now see I missed an opportunity to connect the dots much earlier. Tools like the DSM-5 or National Institute on Alcohol Abuse and Alcoholism (NIAAA) screenings could've helped, but I brushed off the signs, blamed myself, and kept telling myself it wasn't serious.[7]

While this book focuses on helping you recognize real-life red flags and take intentional next steps, I want you to know that professional tools like these exist—and they can help validate what you're witnessing if you need extra confirmation.

At the time, I convinced myself things weren't serious enough to need outside validation. I wanted to believe everything would go back to normal.

For a long time, I didn't feel—or even see—the impact of his drinking. But once I did, I realized something important: alcoholism doesn't become a problem when your loved one says it is. It becomes a problem when it starts taking up too much space in your heart and mind.

If you feel anxious on the way home because you're not sure which version of them you'll be walking into, that's a problem.

If you find yourself walking on eggshells or avoiding conversations just to keep the peace, that's a problem.

If the topic of alcohol plays like a broken record in your mind, stealing your peace and heightening your anxiety, it's time to acknowledge that something deeper needs to be addressed.

Your feelings are valid.

The first time I realized—and actually acknowledged—that I might be facing a problem was on a Valentine's weekend. The kids had gone to their grandparents', giving Steve and me a chance to take a weekend trip with some friends to a local resort. Looking back, I realize now that the shift in Steve's behavior had started days, maybe even weeks, earlier. He was short with me, less affectionate, and more critical. It felt like every little thing I did was wrong. The way I put away the dishes, the show I chose to watch, the way I folded the laundry—he seemed to have a problem with all of it.

I felt like the nitpicking wasn't really about the tasks themselves but about how he felt about me. The tension was thick. There was an elephant in the room. Steve knew I was upset, too, but neither of us addressed it.

I found myself walking on eggshells, feeling lonelier than ever in those moments. Yet, I kept telling myself it was just stress.

The car ride to the resort was tense. Steve took a few jabs at me, complaining that I was on my phone, even though the car was silent, because he was irritated by my choice of music. I told myself it would get better once we arrived.

Within an hour of checking in, I noticed Steve was drinking more than usual. That familiar gut feeling started to creep in—something was going to happen.

We continued with the evening, but the more Steve drank, the harder it became to ignore. He was loud, pounding shots of vodka, and accusing me of flirting with a man at the pool. He even confronted the man, telling him not to talk to me.

Finally, I snapped.

"Steve, if you weren't drinking so much, you could see there's nothing going on here. You're always drinking, and you're delusional."

I watched his face flush with anger. He erupted, yelling at both of us. His friends tried to step in and calm him down, but now Steve was embarrassed—and that only made him angrier. He became so loud that a staff member came over and asked us to leave.

In that moment, I realized Steve wasn't the same person I married—not when he was drinking. All rationale seemed to go out the window. I didn't know what he was capable of when he was out of character.

The car ride home was painfully silent. But before the silence, Steve gave me a thirty-minute rant about how I needed to mind my own business when it came to his drinking, how I had ruined the trip by flirting, and how I was boring and didn't understand how to have fun.

I was so hurt that he saw me differently—in a way he never had before. As crazy as it sounds, I actually blamed myself.

The rest of the car ride was silent, so I turned my focus inward. What could I do to fix this?

If I knew then what I know now, that conversation would have played out differently in my mind. It would have gone something like: Steve's drinking is really ramping up. I'm not to blame for this situation. I need to talk to a counselor about what's happening.

But I didn't have the internal strength at the time. I was blindsided by the sudden change in behavior. I was still in denial. But deep down, I knew this was only the beginning. The red flags were easy to brush off at first. But looking back, I realize they weren't just subtle signs. They were alarm bells I didn't want to hear.

After that weekend, something shifted. I was no longer just Steve's wife—I had become the barrier between him and his vodka. I wasn't his partner anymore. I was a threat.

The truth is, red flags don't always show up bright and loud. Sometimes they look like a glass of water that turns out to be vodka. Other times, it's hidden bottles under the sink, a shift from beer to hard liquor, or a bank statement full of liquor store charges.

Then there are the behavioral signs—irritability, irresponsibility, disrespect. It builds slowly. And if you're not careful, you start adjusting to the chaos as if it's normal.

That weekend was the first major red flag I truly saw, but it wasn't the first one that existed. I had missed many. And the more I ignored them, the more they stacked up.

What started small quickly turned into bigger issues: the argument at the resort, the loss of a job he loved, and eventually, abusive behaviors that forced me to get a restraining order. This is the nature of a progressive disease: it doesn't remain small.

As I began to make sense of what had been happening for so long, I learned something that changed everything: there were actual tools that could help me see the truth I'd been missing.

To recognize patterns of alcohol use, you can look for red flags, but tools like the DSM-5 and the Behavior, Appearance, Mood, and Speech (BAMA) method can also help.[8] Websites like the NIAAA offer quizzes that guide you through identifying alcohol use disorders. Based on the number of symptoms identified, a person can be categorized as having mild, moderate, or severe alcohol use disorder.[9]

Unfortunately, I didn't know about these tools until much later in Steve's disease. By that point, his alcohol use would have been classified as severe. Reflecting on our relationship, I'm struck by how quickly things progressed. In just a few years, we went from subtle signs to being in the thick of chaos. From the glass of "water" to the fight at the resort, from job loss to abuse—each red flag was a step down the same path.

I didn't keep track of the signs I was seeing, and I relied on my relationship with Steve and the trust I had in him as my compass. That compass kept me in denial far longer than it should have. When I asked questions, I was shot down or minimized. I rationalized by thinking, "Well, everyone drinks, don't they?"

But once you start trusting your feelings and instincts—when you reflect on behaviors and the things you see in your home—you begin to recognize these signs. And the sooner you do, the better.

Recognizing these flags is just the beginning. What I didn't realize at the time—and what you need to know now—is that behind those red flags are powerful triggers silently fueling the problem.

The next step is understanding that these issues don't exist in isolation. Addiction is often fueled by hidden triggers, and learning to recognize them is crucial for helping your loved one move toward recovery. Triggers come in many forms: a sight, an event, a smell, or an emotion. We all experience triggers, but for someone struggling with addiction, they can be especially overwhelming.

Even if you aren't an alcoholic, you know what it feels like to be triggered. Maybe you're on a diet and see a commercial that makes you crave that chocolate bar hidden in the pantry. Emotional triggers work the same way, whether it's sadness, stress, or celebration.

For someone struggling with alcoholism, those triggers can be overpowering. I've been guilty many times of using my emotions as an excuse to eat more sugar, and it didn't necessarily have to be a sad event. I've used food to celebrate happy occasions, and when I was feeling down, I'd reach for a bag of chips and eat the entire thing because I was triggered emotionally. This same cycle is true for your loved one.

Some triggers are obvious—like a Budweiser commercial or a friend who pops over with a six-pack. Other triggers are more subtle. One of them is smell. My husband once mentioned that a certain scent reminded him of his favorite drink.

Another less obvious trigger is the time of day. If your loved one is trying to cut back on drinking, you might notice they struggle more at a certain time they'd usually reach for a drink. For Steve, it was around 5:00 p.m. That time had been part of his routine for so long that simply reaching that hour triggered a strong urge.

Some of these triggers we can minimize, and some we cannot. We can't erase a smell from the air, but we can create new habits around tough moments of the day, like going for a walk, helping to reduce stress, or simply distracting them with something positive until the craving passes. Cravings often come in waves, just like emotional food cravings.

While some triggers are obvious, like going to a bar or a party centered around alcohol, others are emotional and less visible. Emotional triggers can happen when a person's emotional needs aren't being met, like when they feel lonely, unseen, or invalidated.

If your loved one feels like a failure in your relationship—or in life—they may think, "I really messed up. You already think low of me, so I might as well do what I want and have a drink." They rationalize their drinking as a way to escape those painful feelings, and the urge becomes stronger.

As you recognize the red flags in your own life—the changes that keep appearing in your relationship with your loved one—you'll eventually reach a point where you feel like you're at a crossroads, asking yourself, "Is it time to intervene here?"

If your loved one isn't ready to admit there's a problem or take action, you'll likely hear them say they need to be ready first, and surprisingly, some health professionals may echo that same narrative.

"I need to be ready in order to go to treatment. I need to be ready, and I need to want it for myself. That's the only way it will work. Until then, give me space and time until I'm ready."

I see this as an old-school way of thinking. We already know—based on research—that early intervention is key when treating this disease, and late intervention is proven to have grim outcomes.[10] So why are people still buying into this narrative?

I know I bought into it for a long time for a couple of reasons. First, I still trusted my husband, and our relationship dynamic was that he was the decision-maker. I looked to him to make financial decisions, parenting decisions, and to lead our household. So, it felt natural to also let him take the lead on whether or not he needed treatment.

Even when Steve was at his lowest point and wouldn't stay in treatment—though I knew he needed to be in treatment—I actually heard from a counselor that he needed to be the one to be ready. I thought to myself, "Okay, if I'm hearing this from him and from a licensed counselor, then it must be true," but this is a dangerous mindset. Most counselors do not advise waiting, but you will still find a few who hold this outdated way of thinking.

When someone is deep in addiction, they are not thinking clearly. They may want to feel better, but they don't want to quit drinking—and they definitely aren't making the best decisions for their health. That's why it's so important to understand that someone doesn't have to be "ready" to begin recovery. Waiting for that perfect aha moment can lead to heartbreaking consequences—because that moment may never come.

Think about it like this: if your loved one were diagnosed with Stage One cancer, and the doctor said, "This is aggressive and fast-moving," would it make sense for them to respond, "I need time to process this. I'm not ready to accept that I have cancer, so let's hold off on treatment"?

Sounds crazy, right?

Cancer spreads. It invades the body, takes over organs, and leads to death if left untreated. Alcoholism is also a progressive disease. It doesn't stay still. It grows—damaging your loved one's body, their mind, your relationship, and your family. And if you wait too long, it can destroy everything.

Now, here's the part that's crucial: your loved one likely does want to get better, but they don't know how. They may be scared, ashamed, or overwhelmed. If you were diagnosed with cancer, you wouldn't know all the answers either. You'd need help navigating your next steps—and it would be hard.

Alcoholism is a chronic brain disorder, and it's also a mental health condition. That means decision-making is even harder.[11]

In fact, alcoholism affects the prefrontal cortex—the part of the brain responsible for judgment and self-awareness. If that part of the brain is impaired, then, of course, they don't see the problem. That's not denial out of defiance; it's denial caused by brain changes.

Your loved one is also physically and psychologically dependent on alcohol, so their brain has become accustomed to using it as a coping mechanism. This only makes it harder for them to recognize the issue.

Now, imagine you have a problem in your own life, like not exercising enough. Maybe your doctor just told you that you have high blood pressure and recommends lifestyle changes: less sugar, more vegetables, and an hour of exercise a day. But life is overwhelming. Between work, kids, and everything else, you don't have the energy. You feel guilty, but you keep falling back into old habits because it's all just too much.

Now imagine someone close to you sees this and says, "You need to fix this now." To them, it's urgent and concerning. But to you, it feels like an overreaction because you don't see the full scope of the problem, at least not yet.

That's exactly what it's like for your loved one. They may not see their drinking as a problem, or at least not one that requires immediate action. And even if they do, they likely don't see it the way you do.

Will they ever recognize it?

It's possible—but only once they're in treatment and no longer using alcohol to cope. That's when things often start to become clear. Once they begin to see the full scope of their drinking and the harm it's caused to themselves and everyone around them, they may finally become receptive to change—and want to continue the journey toward recovery. And this is how change happens.

Are you afraid of taking action too soon?

I was. I was afraid of pushing my husband away. I knew things were already strained because he was aware that I knew about his alcoholism, and the tension was palpable. He felt shame, so he distanced himself from me. I feared he would ask for a divorce if I pushed too hard. I knew the pull of alcohol was so strong that if he had to choose between it and me, it would be no contest.

There was a time, after Steve left the hospital and had his first month-long stint at Betty Ford, when he refused to go back into treatment. I tried to push him, and his reactions were strong. I felt the repercussions immediately. He would manipulate me into thinking I was blowing it out of proportion or make me feel guilty for even bringing it up. His emotional and physical distance afterward felt like a direct threat to our relationship.

I allowed those fears to take over, and I didn't stop to ask myself if I was being rational. Looking back, I cringe. I'm embarrassed by how I thought and reacted at the time. The person I am today is strong enough to recognize that I wasn't thinking clearly. But at that time, that was who I was. These are normal feelings to have in that kind of situation.

Would I have experienced a different outcome if I had a different narrative in my head? It's possible. But I did the best I could with the knowledge I had at the time.

I encourage you to pause and ask yourself if you're being rational. If your loved one's words are making you feel like you can't speak up, it may be time to talk to a counselor or someone you trust. I stayed silent for too long, but you don't have to. If you're feeling like you're ready to encourage your loved one to take the next steps, just remember: You don't have to have all the answers, you're not alone, and don't give up.

Have you ever heard the saying, "Choose your hard"? Life is full of hard choices, and this situation is no different. Both paths will be hard. Convincing your loved one to get into treatment is hard, and stepping away from the situation or staying silent is also hard because you care deeply about this person. They are a big part of your life and will remain that way, whether you take a step back or step forward beside them. The rewards of stepping forward are so much greater, and with the right tools and steps in place, there is hope for a positive outcome. You both deserve a life that doesn't include constant turmoil, and there is a way to make that happen.

I want to share some tools with you that can help with that. Over time, as I began to recognize the red flags and came to the painful realization that my husband fit the criteria for severe alcohol use disorder, our lives felt increasingly chaotic. It was a truth I could no longer ignore, and yet, it was a relief in some ways because at least I had a name for what was happening. But that relief came with its own weight—a steep hill to climb.

I didn't realize this at the time, but my kids picked up on all the red flags long before I did. My son, in particular, carried the heaviest burden. He became my other hand, stepping into responsibilities no child should have to carry. While I sat vigil in the hospital with Steve, my son took on the role of dad for his sisters during a time when his dad couldn't be that person. He cleaned up after Steve's messes and even stepped into the middle of heated situations to try to keep the peace. He acted as the man of the house in so many ways, giving up time with friends to hold our family together during the chaos.

Looking back, I can see how much he endured and how he tried to manage it all. I was too overwhelmed to fully realize the emotional toll it was taking, but I know now that his sense of responsibility was difficult for him.

It was years later that I learned this, but all that time I spent thinking that the younger kids didn't know what was going on—just because the alcohol bottles were hidden—I was wrong. They somehow knew they were there. I added to their confusion by not confirming what they saw. But the truth is, kids sit back and silently watch, observing our every move. It turns out they know more than we give them credit for.

The chaos didn't just affect me; it was taking a toll on the kids as well. They became increasingly anxious, and it manifested in different ways. The baby cried more frequently, as if sensing the tension in the air. My daughter became overly attentive to her dad, trying to anticipate his needs or calm any brewing tension, while my son mirrored her efforts.

What I saw at the time as a close bond between siblings was really their way of rallying together to navigate the turmoil, trying to care for their parents and stabilize the household. They were forced into roles far beyond their years, stepping in as the adults in a home where calm and security had been replaced by unease.

I remember feeling an overwhelming mix of emotions: anger, frustration, but mostly a deep sense of helplessness. It was like being on a roller coaster that I couldn't get off of. One moment, I thought things would be alright and that we would all be okay, and the next moment, I was back to questioning everything.

But even with my head in the sand, I knew the truth: our lives were in turmoil, we were up shit creek without a paddle, and the situation wasn't getting better on its own.

I know how terrifying it is to realize that your loved one's drinking is no longer just their problem. It affects you, your family, and everything you hold dear. It can feel like free-falling without a parachute, unsure of what to do next or how to make sense of what's happening. If you've been questioning your feelings or dismissing your experiences, I want you to know you're not alone.

In the next chapter, we'll take a closer look at these red flags and the broader impact of alcoholism on the family. You'll begin to see how these patterns unfold and why taking action early is so critical. Through my story, I hope you'll feel seen, understood, and validated—and ready to take those first steps forward.

Reflection Journal
Take a few moments to reflect:

- Have you ever questioned your gut instincts when you knew something was wrong?

- Have you noticed red flags but pushed them aside—or blamed yourself instead?

- Are there subtle red flags—like tension at home or mood changes—you've been ignoring?

- Do you feel like your loved one's drinking has started to affect your mental health, robbing your joy, even though they insist everything is fine?

- Have your children started to notice the things you try so hard to cover up? If so, how are they coping?

What are your thoughts? Write them freely. Don't worry about spelling or grammar. This is for you. Just be honest. Let this be your safe space to acknowledge what you've been feeling and seeing. Let your clarity start here.

CHAPTER 3

Silent Lies: Denial and Enabling

Denial and enabling aren't always loud or obvious. Sometimes, they creep in quietly, disguised as small acts of protection—covering up for your loved one, telling a blatant lie to keep them out of trouble, or even providing alcohol to keep the peace. It can also be as subtle as rationalizing the behavior, convincing yourself that it's not that bad or that it's just temporary.

One of the clearest examples of my own denial occurred during a trip to Hawaii with Steve and my parents. Steve was nervous about traveling with them, but I didn't understand why. Once we arrived in Maui, things seemed perfect—except for Steve's drinking.

Forget the hotel cocktails—Steve had better ideas: a Costco run. He insisted on stocking up on alcohol, and I agreed to come along. I found myself in the liquor section watching him fill the cart with six half-gallon bottles of vodka, like we were preparing for the end of days or hosting a resort-wide cocktail party. I was disgusted, but I didn't confront him. Denial set in, and I told myself it wasn't a big deal—just vacation indulgence. Everything would go back to normal when we got home. At least, that's what I told myself as I helped unload what felt like a doomsday liquor haul into the rental car.

Back at the hotel, I tried to sneak the alcohol into our room, hoping my parents wouldn't notice. But my dad, ever the perceptive one, later confronted me. In that moment, I did what I had done countless times before: I lied. I told him the alcohol was for a barbecue with locals, trying to downplay the situation. I wasn't fooling anyone, but I kept telling myself it wasn't a big deal. I was stuck in my own denial, hiding the truth from even myself because that was just easier at the time.

Reflecting on that trip to Hawaii now, I see how clearly it exposed my role as an enabler.

By denying the truth, making excuses for him, protecting him, and avoiding the discomfort of confronting reality, I was only helping him stay sick.

It was just one of the many times I rationalized or downplayed his drinking.

Enabling doesn't always look obvious. It can show up quietly in small lies, cover-ups, or excuses. These moments build up over time, feeding into a cycle that can feel impossible to break. It's essential to recognize these behaviors early, before they pull you deeper into the pattern.

I remember feeling so disgusted with myself. I wasn't just ashamed of Steve; I was ashamed of the role I played in enabling him.

This was just one example of how I enabled him. Looking back, I can see the countless times I rationalized his behavior, bought alcohol for him, or made excuses, whether out of denial or fear.

Denial can act as a defense mechanism, shielding us from painful truths we don't feel ready to face. To protect ourselves from sadness, fear, or anxiety, we end up rationalizing, downplaying, or avoiding what's really happening. I wasn't consciously enabling Steve, but by staying in denial, I kept making choices that supported the behavior I wanted to stop. I was trying to maintain peace, but I was helping him stay sick.

The problem with denial is that it keeps you stuck. It's like having a cloud over your head that you refuse to acknowledge. Instead of tackling the problem, denial lets you avoid it—until it explodes. That inner conflict led me to something many people don't talk about: cognitive dissonance, where two opposing thoughts coexist at the same time, creating chaos.

On one hand, I knew Steve had an addiction. I saw the signs. On the other hand, I kept telling myself everything would be fine. To manage the uneasiness, I compartmentalized, burying my head in the sand to avoid confronting it.

I was guilty of compartmentalization. I would go to work every day with a smile, acting like everything was fine. It was like putting our relationship in a protective bubble, pretending his drinking didn't seep into everything else. I was able to separate Steve's behavior from his identity. I told myself, "He drinks a lot, and he's done things I don't like, but as long as he's still nice to me, then we can continue like this because I love him."

It felt like maintaining normalcy, but in reality, it was just another way to avoid facing the truth.

Avoiding the truth is easy when it feels like too much to handle. You might find yourself doing this, too—avoiding talking to friends and family about what's going on, skipping support groups, or not reaching out to a counselor. These things are all so common when you're afraid of the change that could come once you face it.

When we're in denial, it's like we can't quite make ourselves see things for what they really are—the things that are so obvious to others. Denial often starts as self-protection, but over time, it turns into self-sabotage.

Sometimes, denial sounds like "This is just a bad day" or "Things will go back to the way they were soon." Other times, it looks like burying yourself in work or avoiding family and friends just so you don't have to explain what's really going on at home.

Let's pause for a moment of reflection.

Grab a journal or notepad and take a few minutes to reflect on recent moments where you might have unknowingly enabled a loved one's behavior. This doesn't mean you have to be hard on yourself. It's about awareness.

Ask yourself:

- Did you provide money, knowing it might go toward their habit?

- Did you cover for them, perhaps lying to someone or making excuses for their actions?

- Did you avoid confrontation to keep the peace, even if it meant letting something slide that shouldn't have?

- Did you tell yourself, "It's not that bad" or "Things will get better soon"?

- Were you afraid of what might happen if you faced the truth?

Now, take a few minutes to read what you wrote, then ask yourself:

- Was my enabling or denial rooted in fear?

- What did I gain in the short term? Less tension, a quieter day, temporary relief?

- What did it cost me in the long term—emotionally, mentally, physically?

- How has this affected my relationship with my loved one—and with myself?

- In the long term, did it really help? Or did it keep me stuck in a cycle?

This isn't about perfection. It's about recognition. It's about acknowledging our role so we can allow change to begin.

The Guilt That Follows

I've experienced this firsthand, and I've seen it in others many times as well. One of the most painful components of this is the guilt that comes with it. The guilt can stem from not having the boundaries to say no to something you didn't feel comfortable doing or from later reflecting on a conversation and realizing that, in that moment, you were enabling the very behavior you were trying to stop.

You might notice something else that happens when we unintentionally—or sometimes even intentionally—aid our loved one in their addiction. The impact can go beyond just your loved one and your emotions. There's a domino effect that starts to affect other areas of your life.

I saw this with my daughter when she came to me, telling me she no longer felt safe in the home. That was a wake-up call. It made me realize that enabling doesn't only affect the addict. It affects everyone around them.

The Physical Toll of Enabling

Enabling can also affect you physically, and the consequences are far-reaching. Some of the things you might notice in yourself include:

- Stress and anxiety
- Insomnia
- Fatigue
- A weakened immune system

Stress isn't just something that makes you feel bad or causes poor concentration. It can actually lead to health problems that manifest as disease. The constant emotional strain of living in the cycle of addiction can affect your body in ways you may not even realize at first.

When you're lying awake at night, worrying about what's going on, or waking up throughout the night, that anxiety and stress can lead to insomnia. You might find it difficult to fall asleep, or you might find yourself tossing and turning, unable to get that restful night's sleep you need to face the daunting tasks of the next day.

Over time, you're drained and running on empty, finding it difficult to function during the day. With poor sleep and constant stress, you'll likely feel exhausted—which is not sustainable, day after day.

It can make it hard to get through your workday, engage with your children, or even manage everyday tasks. The fatigue can become overwhelming, leaving you feeling like you're barely getting by.

Stress also weakens your immune system. You might notice that you're getting sick more often. You may find yourself calling in sick to work or feeling physically unwell more frequently. When your body is under constant emotional and physical stress, it becomes more vulnerable to colds and other illnesses.

These are just a few ways emotions can manifest physically. You might begin to see the domino effect—how this issue not only affects your emotional well-being but also your physical health. The cycle takes a toll on everyone in your life, including you.

Reflecting on our role in enabling and acknowledging our part in this isn't about blaming ourselves. It's about awareness.

The more honest we can be with ourselves, the more power we have to change the trajectory and begin healing.

At the time, I couldn't see it for what it was. Awareness—eyes open—is where change starts. Reflection opens our eyes to patterns we couldn't, or didn't want to, see before. And once our eyes are wide open to the truth, we start seeing it all around us, too.

A Mirror in Someone Else's Marriage

I used to work with one of my good friends at the local college. I think we bonded over the fact that we both had husbands with addictions. She was the only person I ever really spoke to about the issue, and from the moment I met her, I knew we had this unspoken connection—an understanding of each other without needing to say much.

I must have been wearing an invisible sign that said, "Wife of alcoholic here," because on the second day we met, she confessed all her problems to me. Her husband wasn't just an alcoholic. He was also a recreational drug user, with meth being his drug of choice.

I couldn't help but admire her because she still showed up to work every day and did an amazing job, acting as though nothing was wrong. She was always well put together—her long hair, perfect makeup—and I honestly wouldn't have known anything was wrong at home if she hadn't told me.

As I got to know her more, I also spent time with her husband. While I could see my own denial and enabling clearly in hindsight, I began to see hers as well, and I was honest with her about what I observed.

Her husband lived as if he were on some extended "gap year" from college. He came and went as he pleased, spending money freely, even though she was the only one working in their household. Sometimes he'd disappear for days without a word, only to come home like nothing had happened. Other times, she wouldn't say anything at all—just gave him the silent treatment while still cooking his meals and handing over money. Then there were the moments when things exploded into shouting matches. She'd tell him to leave, but he'd respond, "This is my house, too." And just like that, he'd stay.

It's fascinating how we can recognize these patterns so clearly in someone else's life, especially someone we care about—yet we're blind to the same patterns in our own. Her situation was a clear example of both denial and enabling, and she was trapped in a vicious cycle.

Years later, I asked her what her biggest fear was. She admitted that she feared that those few days when he disappeared would eventually turn into months or years, and she didn't want to lose him altogether. But in the process of trying to hold on, she ended up losing herself. Her self-esteem, her sense of worth—bit by bit, it all eroded.

That's one of the most painful parts of being caught in this cycle: You can lose yourself in the process. You lose your voice, your identity, and your confidence, all while trying to put out the biggest fire in front of you. Whether it's a drinking episode, a disappearing act, or emotional chaos, the focus becomes managing the crisis rather than living your life.

In my case, and in the case of my friend, the ripple effect touched every corner of our lives. We thought we were holding it all together —that we had everyone fooled—but the seams were already showing. We just couldn't see them yet

It's important to remember that recognizing these patterns is never about blame, and you should never blame yourself or scold yourself for how you could have done or said something differently. This is just a learning experience, a stepping-stone, so that you can move forward in the best way possible.

In Chapter 8, we'll dive into how to break free from this cycle because there are effective tools and strategies that support the health and well-being you deserve. For now, please keep these reflections at the forefront. We can't control others, but we can control our actions.

Reflection Journal
Take a quiet moment as ask yourself:

- Have you found yourself making excuses for your loved one's drinking, either to others or to yourself?

- Have you covered for them, told small lies, or helped them avoid consequences just to keep the peace?

- Have you ever provided alcohol or overlooked warning signs to avoid conflict or tension?

- Do you feel emotionally or physically drained from constantly managing their behavior or moods?

- Looking back, have you rationalized situations that were clearly problematic?

Now go a little deeper:

- What were you trying to protect by staying in denial?

- What temporary relief did enabling give you—and what has it cost you in the long run?

- How is your energy? Your mental and emotional well-being?

Write honestly and freely. No one else will read this. This is your space to explore your truth, not to feel guilt or shame. Awareness is the first step toward meaningful change.

CHAPTER 4

Emotional Abuse: The Silent Danger

Are you questioning your own sanity? Are you being made to feel like your feelings, your recollection of events, and your version of the truth are all just in your head? Loving someone with alcoholism can mean enduring more than just the drinking itself. Emotional abuse that comes alongside it is a silent danger that is often unspoken.

What No One Talks About

I see this emotional abuse as an umbrella term that includes gaslighting, blame-shifting, manipulation, and minimization. These tactics are used to tear down your sense of reality, causing you to doubt yourself and your concerns so they can continue their behavior uninterrupted.

According to the National Domestic Violence Hotline, gaslighting is a form of emotional abuse that causes you to question your own sense of reality, often by minimizing your feelings or denying events.[12] When this happens over and over again, it becomes difficult to trust your instincts, leaving you feeling confused, over-reactive, or even mentally unstable.

This isn't always a conscious decision. It's more of an instinct. People struggling with addiction may not even be fully aware of how deeply they manipulate or gaslight, but they do know they don't want to stop drinking. They'll often go to great lengths to make sure no one gets in the way of that.

How Addiction Fuels Abuse

Although the disease does not define who your loved one is, over time, addiction will cause changes in the brain. These changes heighten fear, anxiety, and shame, fueling abusive behavior.

When someone is drunk and feeling resentful or angry, those emotions bubble to the surface with no filter. During a confrontation, the danger rises, and the chances of abuse in that moment are high. All of these big emotions can so easily manifest under that umbrella of abuse.

What Manipulation Looks Like

Manipulation is a form of influence, and it's not just confined to this situation. People manipulate in various ways all the time. For example, our kids manipulate us when they fake cry to get a toy in the store or flash that sweet smile they know will melt our hearts when they ask for dessert, even though they haven't finished their dinner. These actions are typically done without the other person being fully aware of it.

People tap into emotions they know will evoke a response, using that to sway someone into doing what they want. Some moments are subtle, like the sweet smile, while others are much more direct, such as making a threat to get compliance.

What Emotional Abuse Looks Like

In this chapter, we'll explore through real-life examples what emotional abuse looks like, why it happens, and how it operates. By understanding these tactics, you can begin to recognize them in your own life. Early recognition is important, but even if it's been happening for years, know that it's never too late to see it clearly and take back your power. You do have that control.

It's not uncommon for a family member living with an alcoholic to experience abuse. Unfortunately, this abuse doesn't always stop with the spouse. It often affects the children as well.

The Statistics

Research shows a strong link between alcohol use and increased conflict within the home. According to the National Institute on Alcohol Abuse and Alcoholism (NIAAA), verbal aggression between partners is nearly twice as likely when alcohol has been consumed in the few hours prior.[13] The American Psychological Association (APA) notes that when alcohol is involved, the risk of physical aggression increases even more—by three to four times if the perpetrator has been drinking.[14]

The Long-Term Impact of Alcohol Use

Alcohol use can seriously impact family stability over time. One study found that just a one-liter increase in alcohol per person was linked to a 20 percent rise in divorce rates.[15] According to the U.S. Department of Health and Human Services, more than 9 percent of people have either lived with or been married to someone who met the criteria for alcohol use disorder.[16] When drinking becomes heavier and more frequent, the risk of violence in the home also goes up.

Perhaps most heartbreaking is the impact on children. The Substance Abuse and Mental Health Services Administration (SAMHSA) reports that substance misuse is present in 40 to 80 percent of families where children experience abuse.[17] These numbers are alarming—but they're also eye-opening.

Gaslighting: A Common Tactic

One of the most common forms of emotional manipulation is gaslighting. In my interpretation, gaslighting is when someone tries to get you to see things the way they want you to see them. They might say something designed to twist your view of a situation, often making you feel like your feelings or reactions are exaggerated. It can also happen when someone flat-out denies things they've said, even though you vividly remember their exact words and know they do too.

If this happens often enough, you can begin to question your own version of reality, leading you to ask yourself, Am I crazy?

It's incredibly frustrating when someone denies something you know to be true, whether that's an event, a conversation, or the drinking itself. So, why does this happen?

There can be many reasons, but often, it's rooted in deep guilt or shame. Owning up to the truth would mean having to face those feelings—and that mirror is painful to look into. If someone isn't ready to take accountability, they simply won't.

Blame-Shifting

Another common form of emotional manipulation is blame-shifting. This happens when someone tries to make you take responsibility for actions they should own themselves. Their version of the story paints you as the one at fault. It might sound like "The kids are stressing me out, so I'm just going to relax and have a beer" or "You accuse me of drinking all the time, so I might as well do it." In these moments, they're shifting the blame to avoid taking responsibility. It creates a distraction and takes the focus off their behavior.

This not only causes guilt and shame for you, but it also creates a sense that you're losing control in the relationship. It's important to understand that this usually isn't about intentionally trying to make you feel this way. Your loved one isn't a bad person for doing this; it's often a defense mechanism they're using because they don't yet know how to face the truth.

Minimization

Minimization is another subtle but damaging tactic. It shows up when someone downplays your emotions with comments like "Oh come on, it's not that big of a deal" or "Is my drinking really that bad? No, it's not. You're overreacting."

At first glance, minimization might seem similar to gaslighting, but there's one key difference: gaslighting is aimed at twisting the truth with the intent to control or confuse. Minimizing, on the other hand, is still a form of manipulation, but it's often less deliberate, which can make it harder to identify and call out.

Subtle but Serious

Gaslighting, blame-shifting, and minimization all fall under the category of emotional abuse. Does that surprise you? It surprised me. I always thought of abuse as either physical or blatantly verbal—insults about someone's appearance, harsh criticism, name-calling, or cursing. But these subtle tactics are also abuse.

Abuse isn't always physical. It can come in many forms. Manipulation, gaslighting, and other emotional tactics can be just as damaging as a slap or shove. Words and manipulation hurt you and your relationship in ways that aren't always visible, but the scars run deep.

When Boundaries Break Down

I was never pushed or hit, but I was in an abusive relationship for years, and I didn't recognize it until much later in my journey. At first, it looked like subtle dismissals—brushing off my concerns, shifting blame, or making me feel like I was overreacting. Then came the rages—shouting, broken dishes, slammed doors. And then, the violence. That's when I finally opened my eyes to what had been there all along.

The truth is, I didn't set boundaries early with Steve. I stayed in denial for so long that we became stuck in our pattern. We had this unspoken understanding: In order to keep the peace, I would go along with what he wanted. I wouldn't ask too many questions about his drinking, and I definitely wouldn't push back.

When Steve was first released from the hospital after his near-death experience and was told he could no longer drink or he would die of liver failure, I started to push back. That was the turning point for us, and that's when I began to see the abuse. I wanted so badly for him to admit the truth, and I wanted his family to recognize how serious things had become. But Steve had his parents convinced that because he was cleared to go home, everything must be fine. That I was blowing things out of proportion.

He had them wrapped around his finger. Because they were also alcoholics, I suddenly had both him and his parents in my ear, insisting I was overreacting and needed to back off. They told me Steve would go back into treatment when he was ready.

I heard this so often that I started to believe it. It sounds insane now, looking back. I can't believe I let myself believe that lie for months, but that just shows how powerful manipulation can be.

When Boundaries Aren't Enforced

The next boundary I drew for myself was that I would no longer go to the liquor store and provide alcohol to my husband, even knowing it would harm him. I hadn't been comfortable getting it for him, but Steve needed me to because, at times, he wasn't physically well enough to make it out of the house. This is when things took a turn, from emotional abuse and manipulation to something more dangerous.

He would go into fits of rage because I was now directly standing between him and alcohol. He would shatter dishes, slash my tires, burn my clothes in the fireplace, and pull my hair. I once woke up in the middle of the night with my hair tightly wound around his fingers while he whispered threats, holding a knife in his other hand.

I believe things wouldn't have escalated to that point if I had recognized the earlier forms of abuse for what they were. At the time, I thought setting boundaries was enough—that just saying the words would spark change. But nothing changed because I wasn't following through.

Without realizing it, I was showing him that I would tolerate whatever he dished out. And in doing so, I silently let him know it was okay to raise the stakes.

If I had said, "Next time you drive drunk, I will call the police" or "Next time you name-call, I'm leaving the room," and then actually done it, I might have disrupted the pattern earlier. But without consequences, the cycle just continued.

I was afraid, and I was stuck in fear. I lived in such a

constant state of anxiety that I didn't slow down long enough to think rationally—to realize that the outcome of doing nothing was far scarier than what might have happened if I had followed through on my boundaries.

The Shame of Speaking Up

It's so difficult to balance mixed feelings—wanting to protect someone while also feeling hurt and ashamed by their behavior. I felt that same way when I covered up for Steve in Hawaii. The last thing anyone wants when they're already going through a difficult time is to deal with judgment from the outside—judgment from friends or family. There's that feeling of "Well, if I don't cover for him, then my family and friends will know. And I'll have to deal with questions or even pressure to leave the relationship."

That same feeling comes up even when you consider sharing what's going on with someone close to you. It's normal. And you're not alone in this feeling—it's just not talked about very often for exactly that reason.

The Reasons I Stayed Silent

The reasons I protected Steve were layered. Sometimes, we do something like this for one reason and sometimes, for many. I really think it depends on the dynamics of the relationship. For me, I was afraid to open the can of worms—period. We hid Steve's disease so well. I was so pleased that I was doing a great job of keeping up the façade—this fake appearance.

It sounds so silly now, but at the time, I was proud of it. Like hiding cookies in the pantry and convincing myself they didn't count because no one could see me eating them. I guess I had the delusion that others couldn't see what I didn't want them to, and if I uttered a word about it or decided not to cover for him, then my cover would be blown.

I also had this pride that I could just handle things on my own: I'm smart and persuasive, and I can handle this disease. There was also the fear that Steve would get angry, and I just didn't want to deal with his emotions at the time. I would rather kick the can down the road. Those are the excuses I gave myself. It's all so easy to do.

The Escalation of Emotional Abuse

I now realize that the emotional abuse had been happening for years, intensifying every time I raised a concern about his drinking. It built so gradually that I couldn't see the full picture at the time.

In Steve's case, gaslighting showed up as dismissal. From the very beginning, he set out to dismiss all my concerns, both big and small. It started when I questioned him about having a beer less than twenty-four hours after leaving the detox center. He downplayed my concerns about his health and minimized the seriousness of his drinking.

When I expressed guilt about making trips to the liquor store for him, he'd brush it off with phrases like "No, you don't. You're fine. You're just making excuses." Or, when I voiced concerns about his health, he'd tell me I was exaggerating. Over time, I began questioning my own feelings, perceptions, and emotions—until I no longer trusted my instincts.

Isolation and Self-Doubt

As my confidence eroded, I started pulling away from friends and family. I told myself no one would understand. Steve had already convinced my in-laws that I was being dramatic about his drinking and health, and they bought into it. That only deepened the loneliness. I began to believe that seeking help would just lead to more rejection, so I stopped reaching out altogether.

Looking back, I understand why. Steve's behavior was a defense mechanism. Dismissing my concerns was his way of protecting the addiction. At the time, it all felt like isolated incidents. But eventually, I saw it for what it was: a pattern of manipulation designed to keep me silent. I wasn't crazy. I wasn't the problem.

When Emotional Abuse Becomes the New Normal

Emotional abuse doesn't always start with obvious cruelty. Sometimes, it begins with subtle shifts—dismissive comments, shifting blame, or downplaying concerns—until those patterns become a new baseline.

I had been right all along. His drinking was harming our family, and I wasn't wrong for feeling like supplying alcohol or covering his lies was enabling the addiction.

These mixed emotions influence nearly every decision you make. They're often the result of manipulation that makes you feel responsible for your loved one's actions. Emotional abuse, like gaslighting, blame-shifting, and minimization, can take root so deeply that it clouds your judgment and wears down your ability to respond with confidence.

The manipulation built so gradually that it felt invisible. But now, I see how much it undermined my reality. Each lie, manipulation, or dismissive remark was a blow to my foundation, and eventually, our entire structure felt unsteady. These small attacks add up until you no longer trust yourself—or anyone else.

And while you might not realize what's happening in the moment, your subconscious does. Emotional abuse wears on the subconscious, leading to invisible—but deeply damaging—mental health struggles.

When Gaslighting Breaks You Down

For me, gaslighting hurt the most. It made me lose touch with reality and eroded my self-esteem. I often questioned if I was the problem.

One of my lowest points came during a particularly intense fight with Steve. We had been arguing constantly about his drinking. The tension built for days until I hit a breaking point. I started hiding his alcohol just to make it harder for him to get to it. I even went so far as to hide it on the roof, knowing he wouldn't be able to climb up there since he had just come home from the hospital.

That move sparked a war in the house—broken glass, cruel words, and total emotional exhaustion.

In the middle of all of it, he looked at me and said, "You know you're going to be the reason I go into withdrawal. I'll die, and the kids will be without a dad because you won't give me what my body needs. I'll be throwing up in a couple of hours, probably have seizures, and I'll die at home, but I'm okay with that."

I could see the exhaustion on his face. He was wearing down, and so was I. He wanted to prove a point, and he was willing to play Russian roulette with his life to do it.

Steve did have seizures that day. My son heard a fall in the bathroom and found him unconscious on the floor. Steve survived, but the emotional toll on all of us was beyond words.

PTSD and the Aftermath

I developed PTSD, an anxiety disorder caused by trauma, which made it hard to trust anyone. I thought, If my husband could manipulate me like that, what makes anyone else safe?

With that PTSD came anxiety, depression, panic attacks, and deep loneliness. I felt like I had no one to go to. Panic attacks sent me to the ER. The trauma shattered any trust I had left. Reaching out for help became harder. I was stuck in fight-or-flight mode, overwhelmed by everything around me.

I started blowing off plans and withdrew from my support system entirely. Survival mode became my way of life. The longer I stayed silent, the more impossible it felt to speak up. I didn't even know where to start. So, I told myself to just stick it out, not knowing how—or if—I'd ever break the cycle.

But if no one else has told you this yet, let me be the one to say it: You're not crazy. You're not overreacting. And you're definitely not alone.

I know how heavy this can feel. I know how hard it is to admit what's really going on, especially when you've been holding everything together for so long. But you don't have to keep carrying it by yourself.

You're already doing the hardest part: facing it. And that counts for something.

And if you're reading this in your car or late at night, trying to find answers—wondering if any of this actually gets better—just know: I was there, too.

I used to go on long drives and cry. I forgot to eat. I screamed into a pillow more than once. But I made it out. And you can, too.

You don't have to fix everything today. You just have to keep showing up for yourself, one honest moment at a time.

Why Boundaries Matter

So, how did we get here?

We understand now why the addict manipulates, but we haven't yet talked about where this all truly stems from. In part, it comes from not setting boundaries.

We all have boundaries—limits we don't want crossed—and so does your loved one. In any relationship, it's crucial to establish those boundaries early and make them clear. Will there be pushback? Absolutely. It's normal for people to test boundaries and try to step over the line. But the key is that it's far easier to stop negative patterns if the other person knows what your boundaries are—and if you hold firm to them.

When you don't set boundaries, you're inadvertently telling the other person that it's okay to continue treating you the way they have been. You're signalling that you accept and tolerate their behavior. And over time, that can escalate. If you allow certain behaviors to slide, you begin to wonder what else you'll tolerate, and that raises the stakes in unhealthy ways. It can also convey the message that you don't value your own worth—a card we never want to show.

What Boundaries Look Like

Setting boundaries doesn't have to be harsh, but it is essential.

It could look like letting your loved one know that you're aware of their actions, such as saying, "I'm no longer cleaning up after your empty beer bottles" or "I won't tolerate name-calling or shouting." It might mean stating that every conversation will begin and end with respect, not blame, and setting consequences for behavior that crosses the line.

And when those boundaries are crossed, there needs to be a consequence, not to punish your loved one but to protect yourself and start creating a new pattern.

A consequence might mean walking out of the room the moment he's disrespectful or raises his voice, refusing to lie to cover for him when his drinking causes issues with work or with family, or not cleaning up the messes, like the empty beer cans he leaves behind.

A boundary with no follow-through is just a suggestion. It's the follow-through that gives them power.

We'll go deeper into setting and holding boundaries later in the book, where I'll walk you through how to create a personal boundary plan that feels empowering instead of confrontational.

It's easy to fall into the trap of painting your loved one as the villain in this situation, but that's not the point of boundaries. The goal is not to demonize but to create a neutral space where both sides can be heard and understood. The aim is for both people's needs to be met.

When we establish healthy boundaries, we set the stage for healthier communication and, ultimately, a healthier relationship.

Functioning in Survival Mode

One of the most difficult parts of loving an alcoholic was the constant unknown.

Every morning, I woke up not knowing what kind of hell I'd endure. Would he break a window? Slash another tire?

The uncertainty became a heavy weight I carried everywhere. It was this unpredictability—along with the direct emotional abuse I endured—that led to the PTSD I later experienced.

Honestly, the emotional rollercoaster—the feeling of constantly hanging off a cliff—was the worst part.

It wasn't just the chaos around me; it was the war inside my head. The endless conversations and arguments replayed on a loop. I constantly asked myself, Am I right in this situation, or is he right? That mental back-and-forth was exhausting.

It was like trying to navigate a storm with no compass, unsure of where I stood—or what was even real anymore.

As the manipulation started small and slowly increased, it became glaringly obvious that it was calculated and blatant. I wasn't just emotional. I was realizing I was in an emotionally abusive relationship. My confused, unstable mindset made it hard to confront the real issue. Every time I voiced concerns, brought up treatment, or said no to something I wasn't comfortable with, he would manipulate me again. That made it nearly impossible to get the help we truly needed.

While it can be difficult to recognize gaslighting in the moment, if this rings true for you if you see yourself in my words—know that your feelings are valid. Your feelings are your feelings, and even when we don't have all the facts, the truth still lies in how we feel. Whatever event happened, it made you feel a certain way, and that feeling is valid.

If you're ever made to feel that your emotions aren't valid, please know you're not alone.

It's easy to internalize these doubts, especially when they come from someone we love. I know firsthand how overwhelming it is to watch someone you love struggle, all while trying to make sense of your own emotions. But believe me when I say you are not alone.

There were moments when I felt completely isolated. But I'm writing to you now because I discovered a vast network of individuals—just like you and me—who are going through the same thing. You're only alone if you choose to be.

You have a voice. And your feelings are valid.

I promise you that if you trust your feelings and stand by them, you will have taken the first and most important step toward change: recognizing the situation for what it is and being willing to do something different.

This kind of change doesn't mean fixing your loved one. It means changing how you show up in the relationship. That might look like no longer covering up for them, finally finding your voice and speaking up, or setting boundaries you actually enforce. It might mean protecting your own mental health, asking for support, or honoring your truth—even when it's uncomfortable.

These are the kinds of changes that create real momentum. Later in the book, we'll dive into practical tools that show you how to make these changes and how to inspire treatment and healing in your loved one without losing yourself along the way.

I often asked myself why it took so long to recognize what was happening—not just how severe the alcoholism was but that I was being manipulated into thinking things were okay. I felt guilty and ashamed over this for a long time.

It took me a while to understand that I had to forgive Steve and give myself permission to stop blaming myself. We do the best we can at the time with the information we have. Most of us aren't out here intentionally making bad decisions—we act with the best intentions for the people we love.

This same truth applies to the addict.

That might feel confusing. On one hand, I'm telling you to look out for signs of manipulation and emotional abuse—that gaslighting is intentionally done to target your emotions and distort your reality. But on the other hand, I'm also telling you that your loved one may truly not mean you harm.

Here's what I'm really saying: your loved one is sick. Your loved one has a mental illness. While that's not an excuse for bad behavior, it does mean that they are coming from a place of desperation and fear. They're not in a good place mentally or emotionally.

With that being said, your loved one didn't set out to hurt you. But sometimes, due to the nature of this illness, that hurtful behavior evolves. It's up to you to set your boundaries—to decide what you will and won't tolerate—and begin responding differently: by protecting your peace, holding those boundaries, and standing in your truth, even when it's uncomfortable.

This is where change begins, not by fixing your loved one but by changing how you show up in the dynamic. Later in the book, we'll walk through practical tools that can help you do exactly that: how to inspire treatment, encourage better outcomes, and protect your own well-being in the process.

Above all, you should never blame yourself.

Manipulation—and emotional abuse in general—can be incredibly confusing because the person doing it isn't always like that. They can also be sweet, funny, and charming. So, it's easy to overlook the gaslighting, the subtle dismissal, or the outright manipulation when it seems small.

It's even easy to forgive a direct insult when that person turns around and apologizes—hugging you, cracking a joke, or acting as if nothing ever happened. All of these mixed signals just put you deeper into that place of confusion.

This cycle, however it might look for you, can keep you hooked in. It makes it incredibly difficult to see how unhealthy the dynamic truly is.

It's easy to cling to those moments of hugging it out, apologizing, or going out to dinner to smooth things over. I watched this cycle with my close friend and her husband. He would disappear for three days on a drug binge, then come home and cook a grand meal, fold the laundry, bake dessert, and buy her a gift. She wanted to put on a face for the kids, but I also saw the way she looked at him when he played the guitar in the living room. She simply saw the man she married and wanted to hold on to that version of him just a little longer.

We've covered so much about how and why these problems arise, and I know firsthand it can be difficult to see the subtle ways manipulation can take hold. This is why it's important not to just rely on what your mind is telling you is true but also to listen to your gut. Your gut will steer you and guide you in the right direction. You have an instinctive voice that leads if you listen to it.

From Awareness to Action

To successfully implement the tools I'm about to share with you, it's essential to have a solid understanding of not only the signs of emotional abuse but also why this disease has the potential to lead to abusive behaviors. Awareness is a powerful first step, and while no one said this journey would be easy, it is possible. The small steps you take, paired with the tools I'll share, have the power to bring about real change—if you commit to putting them into practice. This journey to the other side requires more than just understanding; it requires ending self-blame and instead focusing on your commitment to yourself and being true to your feelings so that you can move forward.

I know firsthand how overwhelming it is to love someone who's struggling. There were times I felt completely alone—but I wasn't, and neither are you.

Now, it's time to shift our attention.

What Comes Next

What do we do next? Now that we understand the problem, what can we actually do about it? We know we can't control the situation, so are there actionable steps we can take to help our loved one get on the right track?

The answer is yes.

We'll get into the practical tools you'll need to handle this later in the book. For now, just know you're not crazy, and you're not alone.

You've already taken the first step by acknowledging the emotional toll this has taken on you. In the next chapter, we'll dive into how your mindset can shift everything, starting with the way you visualize change, act as a steady hand in the chaos, and use your voice in a way that gets heard.

Reflection Journal
Take a few minutes to sit, reflect,
and ask yourself:

- Has your loved one ever made you question what's real and what's not?

- Are there moments when you've second-guessed your version of an event or emotion?

- Do you feel afraid to speak, whether from fear of "rocking the boat" or physical danger that might follow?

Now go deeper:

- What has it cost you emotionally to stay silent?

- What boundaries have you allowed to be crossed in your relationship, and how has that shaped your emotional well-being?

- Have you ever blamed yourself for things you know, on some level, aren't your fault?

- Are you seeing those red flags a little clearer now that you've read this chapter?

Don't worry about finding the "right" thing to say. Just let the words come.

CHAPTER 5

Visualizing Change:
The Power of Mindset Shifts

Every good comeback story has a moment when desperation turns into drive—a drive that forces change.

For me, that moment came when I finally accepted the truth: things wouldn't get better on their own. Steve had become unpredictable, angry, and physically threatening. The abuse had escalated into real danger—smashed dishes, sleepless nights, and terrifying outbursts in front of our children. One night, after a drunken spiral, he threatened to kill himself with a knife. That was when I realized I couldn't trust what he'd do next.

Every day, I woke up wondering if it would be my last day—or his. The fear was intense, and all the while, my children were watching it happen. I knew I couldn't keep this up any longer. Something had to change, and it had to change now.

That's the day I made one of the most difficult decisions of my life. I drove to the courthouse, initiated the restraining order process, and told Steve he had to leave. It wasn't an easy choice, but it was necessary for survival.

And while it felt like the end, it was only the beginning—a turning point in my discovery of tools that would transform the way I communicated with Steve and approached our situation. In moments like these, we desperately seek solutions, but we also feel overwhelmed and skeptical, especially after being let down. I knew I couldn't expect Steve's behavior to change overnight, but I began to understand that my own mindset was one area I could control.

I had always known the importance of mindset and visualization in every other area of my life; this is something I was taught from an early age. So why wasn't I applying it here?

Sometimes we get so caught up in a problem that we can't see the solution that's right in front of us. This realization was pivotal—not just in how I dealt with Steve, but also in how I began to see myself and my role in our journey. I didn't have all the other tools yet to tackle the problem, but I did understand mindset and visualization. So that became the first tool I put into practice.

It's an easy yet powerful way to shift your mindset, one that helps you approach difficult situations with greater clarity. Visualization allows you to create a clear mental map that can lead you to the outcomes you want: peace, confidence, and the strength to take the next steps forward.

Visualize the Moment

Take a moment to think about and write down some of the changes you want to visualize in your interactions with your loved one. Is there a specific way you're currently responding during a conversation, or even an argument, that you'd like to change? Is there something about your approach to communication in general that you want to improve?

For instance, would you like to focus on staying calm so conversations don't escalate into hurt feelings or anger?

It's important to write these things down for a couple of reasons. One is so you can reflect back on them, especially as your goals evolve over time. The other is to see how far you've come and how much you've changed. By writing it down, you're giving yourself a way to track your growth and acknowledge the progress you're making as you become the person who creates change.

Let me show you how you can do this.

Find a Quiet Place

Don't let the outside world in. Find a quiet spot where you won't be interrupted, a place where you can truly let go for a few minutes. Close your eyes, take a deep breath, and allow yourself to relax. With each breath, imagine inhaling calmness and exhaling any tension or worry.

Picture all your tension melting away, like ice on a warm day. For these few moments, you're giving yourself the freedom to just exist in the here and now. There's no need to strive for perfection—there's no right or wrong way to do this, and you can't mess it up.

The goal here isn't to fix everything at once; it's to allow your mind to clear enough that new thoughts and clarity can come through. By letting go of distractions, you're creating space for fresh ideas and solutions to take shape.

Take a moment to think of a situation you'd like to approach differently. Maybe it's a conversation with your husband where you want to stay calm instead of letting emotions take over. Or perhaps you'd like to offer positive reinforcement without letting resentment cloud your words. Whatever the case, visualize yourself in that specific moment. Stay present and focused as you imagine the scene unfolding.

What's happening around you? Where are you? Are you sitting together in the living room, standing in the kitchen, or riding in the car? Picture yourself in this moment as though it's happening right now.

You might notice your emotions stirring. This is natural. Visualize yourself breathing through these feelings, using deep, steady breaths to help regulate your emotions and stay grounded.

Check Your Body Language

Now, consider your body language. What is it saying? Are your arms folded tightly across your chest, signaling defensiveness? Or are they open and relaxed, projecting a willingness to listen?

Body language is powerful. Crossed arms can unintentionally put the other person on edge, while an open posture fosters connection and dialogue. Each time you practice openness, you achieve small wins, building both confidence and connection in these moments.

Speak with Calm and Intention

Next, shift your focus to your tone. What does it sound like? Is your voice calm, steady, and warm, or is it clipped and tense? Imagine your words flowing clearly and thoughtfully, maintaining a tone that encourages openness rather than sparking defensiveness.

Picture the Outcome

Finally, reflect on the outcome you hope to achieve. Are you looking to reduce tension and create a safe space for dialogue? Do you want to encourage collaboration and understanding?

As you picture this scenario, focus on how your approach—your body language, your tone, and your mindset—can positively influence the interaction. Visualizing this allows you to actively shape the dynamic toward a more productive and compassionate outcome.

Imagine yourself calm, confident, and at peace. Picture yourself conveying your thoughts clearly, practicing active listening, and responding thoughtfully rather than reactively throughout the conversation. Visualize it as though it's happening in this very moment.

For example, let's say your goal is to visualize your loved one being open to discussing the possibility that their drinking is a problem. Typically, this is a topic they would shut down immediately, not allowing you to share your thoughts or feelings because they are already defensive and anxious about where the conversation is going.

Visualize this: maybe you're sitting across from them at the table. The house is quiet and free of distractions, and both of you are in a relatively good mood. You take a deep breath, gathering your thoughts. You start the conversation by saying something like "I love being around you, and I truly believe that together we can work through anything. I just want to share a couple of quick things I've noticed and get your thoughts."

Now, focus on your body language. Are your arms open, or are they crossed in defensiveness? Imagine your hands calmly resting on the table, or perhaps you're lightly touching their hand, signaling connection. Your posture is relaxed and leaning slightly toward them to show engagement and care. Your tone is calm, low, and steady, not rushed or confrontational.

As the conversation unfolds, visualize your responses. If they become defensive, imagine yourself pausing and taking a breath instead of reacting immediately. Picture yourself saying something like "I'm not here to judge or blame. I just want to share my thoughts briefly and hear yours. That's all I'm asking for in this moment."

Visualize this conversation ending on a positive note. Imagine both of you walking away feeling heard, even if no solutions were reached. You're not aiming to solve everything at once but to create a small, positive shift. Each time you do this, you're opening the door for future conversations where defenses are lower, and trust begins to build.

Focus on How It Feels

Take a moment to reflect on how it feels to be in control of how you respond. Hold on to that feeling. You should notice a sense of calm washing over you, along with confidence and pride. As you continue to take deep breaths, let yourself embrace the satisfaction that comes from knowing you're in charge of your emotions and your reactions. It's an empowering feeling to make a deliberate decision about how to respond—and then carry it out.

When you find yourself on the verge of an emotional outburst or feel like your emotions are getting the best of you, remember that you have the power to change the course of the interaction. This isn't about being perfect, and it's not about expecting instant results. With regular practice, you'll start to see a shift—not just in yourself but in how others respond to you.

The more you remain calm and composed, the more likely it is that the person you're interacting with will begin to lower their defenses. When they no longer feel attacked, it opens the door for better communication and understanding. Take pride in every moment you're able to stay calm and celebrate those small victories as they add up. Each one is a step toward creating a more positive dynamic.

Putting Visualization into Practice

I know this firsthand because I had to practice it when my life was spiraling out of control. Things at home with Steve eventually reached a critical point where I had to seek a restraining order. Our communication had completely broken down, and my kids and I were in danger. Steve went to live with his parents, and while I could finally breathe a sigh of relief that we were no longer in the direct line of fire, I knew my work wasn't done. I was still committed to helping him get the care he needed.

Even with the restraining order in place, Steve's behavior didn't improve. Living with his parents—and being a thirty-six-year-old man basically in hospice care—didn't seem to faze him. He was still drinking heavily and ignoring medical advice. I realized that external consequences alone weren't enough to spark change. If I wanted to influence him, I needed to start with myself.

That's when a friend suggested something that shifted my perspective: manifesting positive change, not as magic but as a way to visualize and transform myself so I could influence him. I began visualizing the kind of person I wanted to be in our interactions and the outcomes I hoped to create.

Mornings before work were quiet. Some evenings were, too. I carved out just a few minutes during these moments to sit quietly and picture the changes I wanted to make. I visualized myself calm and composed, speaking to Steve with clarity and patience. I imagined not reacting emotionally to his defensiveness but instead staying steady and focused. I watched this scene play out in my mind until it felt real.

Small Shifts, Big Impact

In those last few months before Steve moved out, I'll admit I had stooped to a new low. We were both out of control, and I couldn't manage my outbursts. The arguments weren't just about drinking anymore. They had escalated into something more dangerous. But with Steve out of the house, I finally found the space to regain my footing. I began practicing visualization techniques and noticed immediate changes—not just in how I approached Steve but in how I felt about myself.

When I started visiting Steve regularly with the kids, I felt a sense of calm I hadn't experienced in years. It wasn't just because he was now in a controlled environment. It was because I had changed. Even though we were still having the same conversations—starting with me pressing him about going to treatment and planning for the future—something was different. He was finally hearing me out. For the first time, we could get through a conversation without one of us shutting down or getting upset.

This was the beginning of real change—a shift in the relationship. It wasn't dramatic or overnight, but it was progress. He started making better decisions. I was able to support him without enabling, and for the first time, I felt hopeful. It all began with a simple decision: to visualize the person I wanted to be and take small steps to become that person.

The Power of Cumulative Change

Through this experience, I learned that big change doesn't happen all at once. The disease didn't become a major problem overnight, and neither does meaningful positive change. These efforts are cumulative. They add up. The more you do something, the bigger the impact it has over time. I quickly realized that even modest shifts in mindset can have a significant effect. You don't have to go anywhere or spend a dime, and this simple shift can create a ripple effect that changes everything.

I came to understand that my role wasn't to control Steve and his behavior but to help change the environment around him. By shifting my approach, I gave him the space to lower his defenses. This allowed me to approach him with confidence during the tough moments and conversations. I held the power to respond in ways that made a difference.

A Lasting Practice

Looking back, I can say that visualization helped me become the person I needed to be, not just for Steve but for myself and my kids. When everything was falling apart, this simple practice gave me something to focus on and something I could actually control. And while it didn't change everything overnight, it changed me—and that was a big part of what made real change possible. I still use this tool in my life today.

In the next chapter, we'll dive deeper into problem-solving. I'll show you more tools and techniques to encourage and support your loved one in a way that actually works. I'm genuinely excited for you because combining these new tools with your evolving mindset has the power to create real, lasting change.

You're not doing this alone. We're in this together.

Reflection Journal
Take a few quiet moments to reflect and write:

- If you could redo a conversation with your loved one, what would you say differently?
  (What happened? How did you feel afterward?)

- If you could go back and visualize yourself responding in a calm, clear, and controlled manner in that moment, what would that look like? *(What would you say? How would your tone or body language be different from what it was?)*

- What emotional or physical signs tell you that you're starting to lose your cool and no longer holding it together in the conversation?

- When you imagine yourself showing up as the person you want to be—calm, loving, and clear—how does it feel? *(Do you feel safer? Proud? More in control?)*

- What would it mean for your relationship—and for yourself—if you responded like that more often?

- Is there anything holding you back from trying this? *(For example: "This doesn't work," "They won't listen," or "I can't remain calm.")*

CHAPTER 6

The Power of Positive Reinforcement

What if helping someone you love didn't take an ultimatum, a meltdown, or a miracle but something much simpler?

One of the most powerful tools I discovered—and one that sounds almost too simple to be effective—is positive reinforcement. Everyone likes to feel appreciated, to hear they're doing a good job. Your loved one is no different. Recognizing and reinforcing even the smallest positive actions can have a lasting impact.

This technique, part of the CRAFT method, works by acknowledging small efforts with meaningful praise. CRAFT isn't just a theory—this method is backed by research and proven results.[18] Multiple studies support its effectiveness, including one published in Psychology of Addictive Behaviors, which found that up to 63 percent of people with a substance use disorder entered treatment when their loved ones participated in CRAFT.[19] That's nearly double the engagement rate compared to more traditional support approaches like Al-Anon and Nar-Anon, which focus on coping rather than actively guiding a loved one toward treatment.[20]

You might be wondering why this works, how it works, or even having your doubts. I understand. I had the same questions when I first heard about it.

Why would I want to give praise when I'm angry, and
he's still doing a lot of the same bad behaviors? He hasn't
changed, so what exactly am I supposed to praise? Aren't I
enabling his behavior and sending the signal that it's okay
to continue if I praise him?

The answer is no. Praising your loved one does not encourage
bad behavior; it does the opposite. Positive reinforcement
helps to shift the dynamic, creating a pathway to more
positive behaviors.

It's not always easy to praise someone when you're angry,
but if you watch closely and know what to look for, you'll start
to notice small positive steps. These are the moments to acknowledge and praise.

Your loved one already knows what you think of their behavior, even before you say it. Addiction often creates a re-
lentless cycle of shame and self-criticism—like a record stuck
on repeat. They're often harder on themselves than you could
ever be, constantly reminded of their perceived failures.

What they long for—what we all long for—is to feel loved,
supported, and accepted, to know there's still good in them
despite the challenges they face. When they hear something
positive, it interrupts that negative voice, even if only for a
moment.

Saying something as simple as "I'm proud of you today"
or "Thank you so much for acknowledging my feelings" can
make them feel good. And feeling good is something they
want to experience again.

Positive reinforcement taps into this human need and creates a cycle where they seek more affirming moments. This
technique works because it reinforces the behaviors you want

to see more of. It shows your loved one that their positive actions, no matter how small, are noticed and valued.

Over time, this encouragement helps them build confidence and motivation to continue making better choices.

Positive reinforcement means rewarding the behaviors you want to see more of. It's about focusing on the good instead of the bad. Think of it as a glass-half-full approach rather than a glass-half-empty one.

Rewards can take many forms: verbal praise, planning a date night or cooking a favorite meal. The behaviors you choose to reward will depend on what you want to encourage. For me, I focused on small wins—like showing up for doctor appointments, cutting back on drinking, or being honest with me.

While we all hope for drastic changes overnight, addiction doesn't work that way. Small changes are still big steps forward. For example, if your loved one admits to drinking instead of lying about it, that's a win. Honesty takes courage, especially when they know it might upset you.

Instead of reacting with anger or frustration, take a deep breath and respond with something like "I'm so happy you feel comfortable being honest with me. That means so much, and I'll do my best not to get upset because I want you to feel safe coming to me."

By acknowledging their honesty, you're reinforcing the behavior you want to see more of. You're making future uncomfortable conversations less daunting, which can lead to more open communication and, eventually, discussions about treatment.

Another example might be if your loved one comes home instead of staying out drinking. Even if they're still drinking, acknowledge the effort:

"I'm so glad you came home tonight. It means a lot to me that you're here, and I appreciate you thinking about how I feel."

Small steps like these build trust and encourage continued progress.

It's important to maintain your boundaries, even while practicing positive reinforcement. Abuse of any kind is never acceptable, and if your loved one's behavior crosses a line, it's okay to remove yourself from the situation while still acknowledging their effort.

For example, if your loved one is intoxicated but made an effort to stay home, you could say, "I appreciate that you stayed in tonight. I'm going to spend some time with the kids, and we can talk later."

This approach keeps the focus on their positive choice while protecting your own well-being.

I was floored when I stumbled upon this method. At first, I felt angry. I had been to multiple counselors and doctors, and I had even sent my husband to Betty Ford for treatment. But no one had ever told me how to deal with him when he came home. No one gave me any tips on how to steer him into treatment, keep him in treatment, or what to do when he relapsed. There was no support. I was completely on my own, and it was terrifying.

And yet, here they were—these tools laid out in front of me.

I decided to focus on the positive and be thankful that I had found it at all. As I started researching, one idea stood out to me immediately: the concept of giving positive reinforcement. It felt so different from anything I'd heard before. In fact, it felt revolutionary.

This was a new approach for me, especially because the outside world often sends the message that you should just disengage from your loved one who is using. But disengaging felt impossible; it's not what anyone wants to do when they care about someone. The idea of turning away from Steve was tormenting and heartbreaking. So, this method resonated with me deeply.

I decided to put it into practice immediately and began praising every positive thing I saw. One of the first things I noticed was that Steve had started taking accountability for some of his recent actions and the bad behaviors he'd exhibited before the restraining order. I was still angry and still processing everything he had put the kids and me through that led to him living at his parents' house. But I was determined to give this method a real chance, so I put my anger aside.

When Steve looked at me and apologized, I looked back at him, sincerely, and said, "You apologizing to me really means a lot. I know it must be very difficult for you to recount in your mind what you did and, even more, to own up to it and apologize out loud. That takes courage, and I'm so proud of you for that."

I could tell he was proud of himself in that moment. He felt good, and I could see a small transformation in him. He was beaming that day. It was as though the weight he had been carrying had been lifted, and I gave him the peace to let it go. That moment was powerful, and he wanted to feel that way again.

Soon after, I noticed he wasn't drinking as heavily. To be clear, this didn't mean he was down to one beer a day. Steve was still drinking, just not as much. The same half-gallon bottle that would normally be gone by morning was still there when I came back to visit the next afternoon.

I made a point to let him know I noticed the effort he was making to cut back. I said, "I can see you're making an effort, and it means a lot to me. I want you to know I see it."

It was a snowball effect, and everything began to improve overall. Steve and I were finally able to communicate in a way we couldn't before because he no longer viewed me as someone he needed to fear or avoid. He no longer saw me as the critic. He saw someone who believed in him.

Now that we've learned how positive reinforcement can drive change, let's take a minute to try it out.

Let's Do a Quick Exercise

Write down three small efforts or positive actions you've noticed in your loved one recently. These don't need to be big or dramatic. Small steps matter.

Next, write down how you'd like to respond to each of those positive steps. Think about what you want to say to your loved one to acknowledge and reinforce their efforts.

Finally, commit to saying those words out loud to them.

Remember, this alone isn't a cure. But with a positive mindset, consistent reinforcement, and a loving approach, you'll begin to see changes over time. Be patient and consistent. Progress might not happen as quickly as you hope, but when you look through a positive lens, you'll start to see everything coming together.

In the next chapter, you'll continue building your skills by learning how to help your loved one form new, healthy habits.

Reflection Journal: Practicing Positive Reinforcement
Take a few moments to reflect and write:

- What comes up for you emotionally when you praise your loved one?
  (Do you lack confidence in what you're saying? Do you feel resentful, hopeful, skeptical? Write about where those feelings come from.)

- Have there been moments when you held back praise because you were still upset or frustrated?
  (If so, what would you say now if you could go back?)

- What's one small positive act or behavior your loved one has made recently?
  (It could be honesty, coming home on time, trying to connect with you, or even just being present.)

- How do you think your kind, thoughtful words might affect them emotionally, even if they don't show it right away?

- What needs to shift in you to help you offer praise openly and consistently?

Final prompt:

Write down one positive thing you can say this week to acknowledge even the smallest effort your loved one makes.

CHAPTER 7

From Praise to Progress:
Reinforcing New Habits

Sweet words won't fix dysfunction, but strategy might.

There comes a time when praise isn't enough—when loving words alone can't undo the damage or drive real change. You need something deeper. Something that sticks.

Praise opens the door, but reinforcement is what keeps it from swinging shut again.

In the previous chapter, we explored how recognizing small efforts can begin to shift the dynamic. In this chapter, we'll focus on how to build on that momentum and help those changes last. The goal isn't just to praise your loved one—it's to support them in building a life where positive habits can develop and thrive.

Change happens gradually, and it starts with small, consistent shifts in behavior. As those positive actions are reinforced over time, they begin to replace old patterns.

In this chapter, we'll explore how to help your loved one begin that process—and how your influence can help shape the environment that supports their change.

I understood that in order for Steve's changes to stick, it wasn't enough to just praise isolated actions. I had to help shape the environment around him. That meant paying attention to new behaviors and gently encouraging those things to continue. If he took a small step forward—like delaying drinking to work on his truck or choosing to ride his bike instead of sitting inside—I made sure to acknowledge it in a way that felt genuine, not forced.

This wasn't about pretending everything was okay. It was about creating a space where healthier habits could begin to take root—and in doing so, I was building him up.

For example, if your loved one starts attending one doctor's appointment each week or joins a recovery group meeting without you prompting them, that's progress. Or maybe they start engaging more with your kids—helping with homework, showing interest in their day, or simply being present at the dinner table. These aren't grand gestures, but they're meaningful signs that something is shifting.

It might look like going into the garage and saying, "Wow, this looks great. I'm not as good at organizing, so I'm glad you made a lot of space in here today." Or if he came home from a bike ride, you might say, "How was your ride? I think it's awesome you're getting out there. I need to do that myself—it's been a while." These small, simple affirmations make a difference.

Even something as simple as taking a walk instead of pouring a drink shows they're finding new ways to cope. When you see these new behaviors, acknowledge them with sincerity:

"Thanks for sitting with us at dinner. I know that hasn't been easy lately."

"I noticed you went for a walk this morning. That's a great way to start the day."

These kinds of affirmations encourage more of the same and reinforce that the change is not only possible—it's noticed.

But I need to be honest: I only had a few weeks to put this method into practice. Steve's health had declined so much by the time I started using these tools, and his body simply didn't have time to catch up. Still, in those final weeks, I saw something I hadn't seen in a long time: hope. A shift. Open communication in our conversations.

That's why I believe in this approach—not because it saved him but because it could have if I'd known about it sooner. And that's why I'm sharing it with you. Because if you're reading this, there's still time.

When new habits are introduced into your loved one's routine, they start to replace the negative ones. These shifts might seem small and insignificant at first, but over time, they lead to real transformation. You'll start to notice these changes not only in their habits but also in how they function within your relationship and other parts of their life.

Soon, we'll talk about how you can encourage self-reflection in your loved one using techniques like motivational interviewing. These strategies act as a mirror, helping them recognize that they have a problem and uncover their own reasons for wanting to seek help. With these tools, you'll feel more confident in guiding your loved one toward recovery and healing.

Creating an environment where new habits can take root is powerful. But to keep that momentum going, your loved one needs to feel successful, seen, and encouraged in the moment. That's where timing comes in.

We've talked about the importance of praise, but we haven't yet talked about timing. When it comes to reinforcing new habits, timing is everything. The brain naturally associates actions with their consequences, and the closer the reward follows the behavior, the stronger that connection becomes.

Timing makes all the difference. The brain forms stronger connections when the response to a behavior happens right away. When that reinforcement is repeated consistently, it helps the brain connect the dots and strengthens the new behavior over time.

It's no different for your loved one, especially when they're in the early stages of change. When they make a better choice—even a small one—the closer your positive response is to that moment, the more it reinforces the behavior. That's how the brain begins to associate those actions with positive outcomes: *That felt good. I want to do that again.*

To make the most of these moments, here are a few simple, research-backed ways to reinforce behavior in real time:

Let your reinforcement be immediate and authentic. A kind word, a smile, a thank-you—something that tells them you noticed. It doesn't have to be dramatic. In fact, the more natural it feels, the more powerful it is.

Tools for Timely Reinforcement

1. The Three-Second Rule
   When you notice your loved one making a healthy choice, respond within three seconds. It can be as brief as a warm smile, a "Hey, that's awesome," or a quick "I love you." Even just eye contact with a positive expression goes a long way.

2. A Gentle Touch
   A hug, a high five, or even a quick hand on the shoulder can quietly say, *I see you.* It breaks through the shame without needing a single word.

3. Be Specific When It Matters
   Sometimes a warm smile is enough, but if your loved one changes something you've specifically been struggling with (like coming home late), call it out. Try: "Thanks for coming home on time for dinner. I'm so happy you're here."
   That kind of direct, specific feedback tells them their effort matters.

4. Track It in a Journal
   This isn't just for them— it's for you. Write down the positive actions you noticed and how you responded. Over time, this helps you see patterns, measure progress, and stay encouraged when things feel stagnant. Small wins add up.

Now that you've seen how positive reinforcement can drive change, let's talk about why it works.

When these new behaviors are repeated, they actually begin to rewire the brain. Neuroscience shows that habits form through consistent actions paired with rewards. Every time your loved one chooses to replace an old negative behavior with something positive—like going for a walk or showing up for dinner—they're reinforcing a new neural pathway. Over time, the brain starts to favor that positive pattern instead of the old one.

That's why repetition matters. It's not just about trying harder. It's about changing the brain's natural response.

Creating an environment where new habits can form is powerful, but to keep that momentum going, your loved one has to believe that change is possible—and that it's worth it.

That's where the shift really begins—when they start asking their own questions, not just answering yours to pacify you.

In the next chapter, we'll explore how to help your loved one begin asking the right questions, not just because you want them to but because they sense they can begin to uncover the answers themselves. That's where true transformation begins.

Let's Do a Quick Exercise

Keep Practicing What Works

If you haven't already, revisit the exercise from Chapter 6 where you wrote down three small positive changes you've noticed. Keep using that process—but this time, pay special attention to when you offer your encouragement. The closer your response is to the moment of the positive action, the stronger the impact.

Notice the behavior, respond sincerely, and track your efforts. Consistency and timing are what transform praise into lasting change.

When introducing new habits into a routine, your loved one is replacing negative behaviors with healthy ones, giving their brain the opportunity to rewire. These changes might seem small at first, but over time, small changes lead to big transformations. You'll start to see these shifts not only in their habits but also in how they function within your relationship and other aspects of their life.

In the next chapter, we'll explore how you can encourage self-reflection in your loved one by using techniques like motivational interviewing. These strategies will help them recognize that they have a problem and uncover their own reasons for seeking help. With these tools, you'll feel more confident in guiding your loved one toward recovery.

Reflection Journal:
Reinforcing New Habits
Take a few quiet minutes to reflect and write:

- What new or healthy behaviors have you seen in your loved one lately that you probably didn't notice in the past?
  (It doesn't matter how small—just name a few.)

- What was your initial reaction? Did you respond quickly, or did you let the moment pass?
  (What could you say next time to encourage them more intentionally?)

- How consistent have you been with giving positive reinforcement when something goes well?
  (What's getting in the way? Is it perhaps feeling drained, resentment, or fear that it "won't make a difference"?)

- How do you think your loved one feels in those moments when you acknowledge the effort they made?
  (Do you think it might help keep them motivated, even if they don't say it or show it yet in the way you hope?)

- What do you need in order to keep offering positive reinforcement in a calm, consistent way?
  (Think emotional support, mindset, reminders, or boundaries.)

- What's one positive step your loved one could take this week that you want to be ready to notice and reinforce?
  (Write it down—and be watching.)

CHAPTER 8

Helping Them See It: Guiding Awareness Without Judgment

They're losing everything, but they still think they're fine. Loving someone in delusion is like drowning—screaming, desperate, exhausted, and unheard.

How do I get them to see their drinking Is a problem? If you've ever asked this, you're not alone. It's the million-dollar question that so many people grapple with. You see the obvious: heavy drinking, broken relationships, half-hearted effort in the things that used to matter, and a slow decline in health. But they either don't see it—or can't face how serious it's become.

Sometimes, they know it—but saying it out loud would mean facing it, and they're not ready for that.

What I do know is that getting angry and giving ultimatums isn't the way to help someone reflect on their drinking or acknowledge it. Instead, you need to create a safe space and open lines of communication that allow them to reach that awareness on their own. People are far more likely to take action when they come to that conclusion themselves, rather than having it pushed onto them.

In this chapter, we'll dive into tools and techniques designed to encourage that realization you're hoping for—that moment of self-reflection that can be eye-opening for your loved one. These tools rely on your empathy and active listening to help them develop that awareness on their own.

With time and patience, these techniques can help your loved one take the first steps forward.

So, how do you help someone connect the dots? One of the best ways is by getting them to think about why they drink, not why they started years ago or what trauma may have led them down this path, but what's happening right now that pushes them toward alcohol. This isn't about uncovering deep-rooted pain. It's about creating space for small, honest moments of reflection.

This approach is called functional analysis, and it's not about solving the problem on the spot—it's about planting the seeds of self-awareness. Even simple questions like "What's going through your mind when you pour that drink?" or "What kind of day makes you want to drink more?" can shift something internally.

If your loved one isn't too deep into addiction, these kinds of questions might spark early insight. And if they are further along, it might help them notice what's fueling the binges now—stress, shame, boredom, loneliness. Either way, the goal isn't to fix it. It's to help them pause, think, and notice. Because that's where change begins.

Start by asking questions that aren't loaded or confrontational. This invites your loved one to reflect on what leads to their drinking without feeling cornered or judged. We know that if your loved one is a heavy drinker, their body and mind are likely dependent at this point, but the goal here is to uncover what specifically triggers them to reach for alcohol.

If you lead with a question like "When you come home, what leads you to drink?" It can feel like a trap. Questions like this often put someone on edge, making them defensive and shutting down the conversation. Instead, begin with broader, non-threatening questions that encourage them to open up. For example:

- "When you come home after a long day at work, how do you feel?"
- "Are there tasks at home that make you feel stressed?"
- "Is there a certain time of day when you feel most at ease?"
- "What's the best way for you to unwind when you feel stressed?" Once your loved one answers these questions, you can gently steer the conversation toward more direct, leading questions.

For example, if they say they feel stressed when they come home from work, you might respond with:

"I'm sorry, I didn't realize you felt that way. Why are you stressed when you come home, and what relieves that for you?"

If they mention alcohol as a way to relax, you can validate their experience without judgment:

"It sounds like in those moments, drinking helps calm your nerves and makes you feel better. How do you feel later that night or the next day? Do you feel the same then as you do in the moment?"

This encourages them to think more deeply about the aftermath of drinking. They'll naturally start to recognize that while alcohol might bring temporary relief, it often leads to negative consequences later, whether that's exhaustion, emotional lows, or other struggles.

If they avoid mentioning alcohol and say something like, "I usually call a friend," you can continue exploring with curiosity: "That's great. What else do you do to unwind?"

While both functional analysis and motivational interviewing involve asking thoughtful questions, they serve different purposes.

Functional analysis helps them notice what they're doing and when they tend to do it.

Motivational interviewing goes deeper. It's about helping them uncover why change might matter now.

Motivational interviewing takes things a step further. It's like holding up a mirror, although it doesn't just show them their behaviors; it also helps them connect those behaviors to their goals and the kind of life they want for themselves.

This is where the "why" comes in:

Why do I want to get help? Why do I want a better life for myself?

With functional analysis as a foundation, let's explore some simple motivational interviewing techniques to help them understand why change is important now.

Again, we are not doing this forcefully; we are simply uncovering what's already there.

Let's start by helping your loved one recognize their current situation and see the distance between where they are in life now and where they want to be. For example:

- "You told me earlier that you want to be healthy and to be able to go to the gym again. How do you think drinking aligns with that goal?"

- "You said you'd like to earn more money and get a different job, but you've had some struggles in your current position due to calling in to work and showing up late.

Do you think you'd have the same issue in the next job? How would that be different if you're still drinking?"

Pointing out these problems that they've expressed themselves can help them recognize the need for change.

A good way to gauge your loved one's feelings or pain points is to use scaling questions, which ask them to rate their experiences on a scale of one to ten.

You can use these simple one-to-ten questions in all kinds of situations—work, health, your relationship— to help them start connecting the dots. For example: "On a scale of one to ten, how much do you think drinking plays a role in that?"

Once they answer, follow up with:

"What would help move that number closer to a ten?" or "Is it always a two, or do some days feel worse than others?"

Once they give a response, that's your moment to gently dig deeper and help them reflect. For example: "What would help move that number closer to a ten?" "How did you come up with a two? Would you always rate it that way, or are there days it feels higher?"

These kinds of questions spark the self-reflection you're hoping for. Even if the conversation ends there, chances are they'll keep thinking about it later, quietly unpacking their choices and what's driving them.

If your loved one seems shut down or says they don't want to answer, that's okay. That's normal. This might be the first time they've been asked something this deep, so don't let that discourage you.

What you're doing is laying the groundwork for change.

Even when it feels like they're not listening, they are— they hear you and carry your words with them. The key is to

keep things calm, open, and casual—not intense or confrontational. The more you stay curious, the better your chances
are of opening a real dialogue. And that curiosity? That's what
creates space for self-awareness—one of the most powerful
steps toward lasting change.

I want you to know there's no right or wrong way to do
this. The tools and examples I've shared are just a guide.
What truly matters is that you're opening up the conversation, communicating, and asking questions—any questions
that encourage your loved one to think and reflect. That's the
key: you're moving in the right direction with every question.

Once your loved one begins to open up, the next step is
everything—how you respond can either build momentum or
shut it down.

In the next chapter, we'll talk about how to guide the
conversation forward in a way that helps them consider real
change—without pressure, control, or ultimatums. Let's dive
into this together.

CHAPTER 9

Guiding Without Controlling: Introducing the Idea of Treatment

I sat across from him, sobbing. I couldn't keep my composure. I had carefully rehearsed exactly what I would say—how I would beg him to go back into treatment and stay for the full time, just like they'd recommended. I thought maybe, just maybe, he'd feel some compassion for me. That he might do it for me.

But he looked at me, emotionless, and said, "No. It's over. I'm not going back."

I felt so defeated, but something also shifted. That moment didn't make me give up, but it did make me pause and regroup. I knew I had to try a different way. What I was doing wasn't working, but I believed there had to be a method or resource I hadn't uncovered yet. Pleading and pushing weren't working. If anything, they were making things worse.

Maybe you've been there, too, doing everything in your power to help, only to be met with resistance or silence. It's exhausting. That moment was when I realized that if I wanted to make progress, I had to change my approach.

That's when I started learning how to gently guide instead of push. After planting seeds and focusing on self-reflection, the next step was helping him take action.

When I say "gently," I mean approaching these conversations without demands, ultimatums, or pressure. This is exactly where the CRAFT method comes in. One of its core principles is learning to influence change through encouragement instead of control. It's not about giving up; it's about changing how you show up.

That shift in approach is exactly what the CRAFT method teaches. You're not backing down; you're shifting to a new strategy. CRAFT gives you tools like positive reinforcement, open-ended questions, and reflective listening to help your loved one feel supported, not attacked. You're not demanding change; you're helping them explore the idea of change in a safe way.

You want to introduce the idea that they don't have to go through this alone in a supportive, loving way. The goal is to make the idea of treatment or reducing drinking feel like a natural, approachable next step. That's what guiding without controlling really looks like. You're opening the door, not shoving them through it.

I know these conversations can feel daunting, especially when you've had them before, and they didn't go well. You might feel scared to try again or wonder if it's even worth it. That fear is valid. But you've got this.

A helpful way to prepare for these conversations is to role-play. I know it might sound silly, but practicing what you're going to say can make a big difference. Getting the words out beforehand helps you feel more confident and relaxed when the real conversation happens. Planning helps you stay calm and ensures you don't come across as overly intense or emotional, which could make your loved one shut down. These tools can feel awkward at first, which is exactly why it helps to practice, whether it's with yourself in the mirror or with a trusted friend.

Here's an example of how one of these conversations could go:

> "I've noticed you seem down lately. You're not doing the things you used to enjoy, and I know you want to feel good again."

If they respond with something like:

> "Yeah, I've just been depressed lately, and I don't know why," you could follow up with:

> "I'm sorry you're feeling that way. I've dealt with those feelings myself, and I know how hard it can be to pull yourself out of it. Have you thought about talking to someone about this?"

This approach keeps the focus on their feelings, creating an opportunity to introduce the idea of getting outside help without directly confronting the drinking.

Another way to approach the conversation could sound like this:

> "Hey, I've noticed you've been really stressed lately. Is it work, or is something else going on at home?"

If they reply with:

> "Yeah, everything just feels overwhelming right now," you might respond with:

> "I completely understand. I've been through those times too, and I know how hard it is. Maybe talking to someone could help manage that stress. What do you think?"

These conversations plant the idea that they don't have to live with the stress or depression they're experiencing and that support is available. It's not about forcing the topic of treatment but rather introducing the concept in a way that feels safe and approachable.

Keep in mind that not every conversation will go the way you want it to. Your loved one might become upset or deny needing outside help. Don't worry—this is a normal response. Just remain calm, even if you feel you're at your wits' end. Take a deep breath and keep your composure.

Your loved one might say:

"There's no problem here, and I don't need to talk to anyone."

You could respond with:

> "I understand, and I hear what you're saying. I just want you to know that I'm here to help. I want you to see the opportunities and the support you have around you."

This kind of response removes pressure or tension from the conversation. It shows your loved one that they are supported, and it leaves the door open.

Or they might say:

> "Why would I go to treatment when I already know it won't work?"

At this point, Steve had nothing. No job and no possessions except the bag he had brought to his parents' house. The home he helped pay for, the furniture we picked out together— everything he had built was gone. He had no control.

I truly believe he was at a crossroads, questioning if he even wanted to continue with his life.

Steve was in hospice care due to his heavy drinking and the devastating effects of liver disease. The reality of his situation was inescapable: he had a choice to make, and it needed to be made now.

As we sat there, I took a deep breath and said to him:

> "I know you're not happy right now, and I understand that. It doesn't have to be like this. Are you ready to go back to treatment and get help?"

It was so difficult not to say more in that moment. Of course, I wanted to burst into tears—I had been crying privately every day, multiple times a day, for months. But I couldn't let myself break down in front of him. This moment wasn't about me.

Steve asking to come home was Steve asking for help. He didn't say those exact words, but I knew what he meant. He didn't want to live like this anymore. He wanted things to be as they once were.

Did I want that? Of course I did. I desperately wanted to wave a magic wand and make it all better.

But deep down, I knew what would need to be in place for that to happen.

Steve needed to commit to a long-term treatment facility. He needed to accept the help being offered and give himself fully to the process the professional counselors had laid out for him. There was no other way.

When I asked if he was ready, his response was positive. He agreed to go into treatment.

There was no tiptoeing around the topic of treatment this time. No code words or careful phrasing. When I asked him if he was ready, he didn't hesitate or deflect—he answered me directly and without excuses. That's where we were in this journey. It was literally do or die.

In that moment, I felt an overwhelming sense of relief and deep emotion. This was what I had been fighting for. I had endured so much to get to this point. Our journey wasn't over, but this was a turning point in our lives together.

It's moments like these—even if they aren't catastrophic—that can serve as turning points. Everyday moments, like watching the kids play or sitting together after a long day, can create opportunities for these conversations. The more you approach your loved one in a casual, supportive way, the more open they'll be to considering treatment.

It's important to remember that treatment can feel like a big, scary commitment for them. It might take several conversations to warm them up to the idea, but every small step counts.

Active listening is key. Hearing their struggles—whether it's stress, depression, or feeling stuck—will bring you closer to helping them consider treatment. Even if your efforts seem small, they're making an impact.

These tools and techniques are planting seeds, and over time, those seeds will grow into meaningful change.

If you've been doing your best to stay patient and calm, I want you to know that you're doing an amazing job. You're coming from a place of love and support, and as long as you're doing that, you're already on the right track. Give yourself some grace. This path isn't easy, but with each conversation you have with your loved one, you'll inch your way toward change.

Whether your goal is to encourage them to cut down on drinking or take that step toward treatment, the key is to keep that door open for change. You're creating a space where change feels achievable—and that's a powerful step forward.

In the next chapter, we'll dive into the CRAFT method with Michelle Kuecker, a CRAFT method expert and licensed clinical social worker. Michelle shares her perspective on

CRAFT techniques, along with additional messages of hope and support. Her advice will be a wonderful addition to your approach, giving you even more confidence to put these techniques into action. I'm so excited to share her knowledge with you.

Reflection Journal:
Encouraging Action Without Pressure
Take a few quiet moments to reflect and write:

- What fears come up for you when you think about bringing up the topic of entering treatment or quitting drinking?
  (Is it fear of hearing something that will upset you, fear of anger, or worry that you'll make things worse?)

- Have you ever tried to talk about entering treatment before? How did it go?
  (What happened?)

- If you could go back and redo one of those conversations, how would you approach it differently?
  (Think about your tone, timing, body language, and the words you used.)

- What's one supportive phrase you could use to start a new conversation about getting help without putting your loved one on the defense?
  (Write out one sentence you can try.)

- When it comes to the conversation itself, what would you consider a win, even if it's just a small step?
  (It could be them staying calm, listening, or even just not leaving the room.)

CHAPTER 10

Expert Insights:
Conversations That Inspire Change

Craft in Action: Real Stories and Professional Tools

This chapter brings together two perspectives that complement each other so well: those of Jane Mackey, the founder of We The Village, and Michelle Kuecker, a licensed clinical social worker and certified CRAFT practitioner. Together, they offer the perfect combination of personal experience and professional expertise, showing how the CRAFT method truly transforms lives.

What Is the CRAFT Method?

CRAFT, which stands for Community Reinforcement and Family Training, is a proven method designed to help family members encourage a loved one's recovery from substance use—without pressure, conflict, or cutting ties.

Instead of using control or ultimatums, CRAFT leads the way—showing you how to stay connected and guide your loved one toward treatment in a way that actually works.

This method focuses on:

- Positive communication:
  You'll learn to communicate in a way that keeps the

conversation open instead of your loved one shutting you down.

- Reinforcing healthy behavior
  CRAFT helps open your eyes to even small positive steps your loved one is making and encourages more of them through your positive reinforcement.

- Reducing unintentional support:
  You'll start spotting ways you might be unknowingly supporting the addiction—and how to avoid doing it.

- Setting healthy boundaries:
  Without being cold or tarnishing your relationship, you'll protect your peace and clearly state what you're no longer willing to do.

- Self-care:
  This method reminds you that focusing on your health and well-being isn't selfish—it's necessary.

What I love most about CRAFT is that it provides a guide to follow, actionable steps, and it empowers you. You don't have to sit back in agony and wait for things to get worse. You can take action now—thoughtful, steady, compassionate action that makes a difference.

Everything Jane and Michelle share in this chapter is built on this method, and by learning about it, you're already one step closer to change.

Jane's story is one of commitment and love, and her journey has gone on to transform the lives of thousands through her advocacy work and research. As the founder of We The Village, she has created programs that empower families with tools proven to help navigate addiction recovery.

When I spoke with her, it was clear how much her insight comes from personal experience and her genuine desire to share what she's learned so others can find success too. Michelle brings a professional perspective, having worked directly with addicts and their families. As a licensed clinical social worker and certified trainer for Dr. Robert Meyers, the founder of the CRAFT method, she works tirelessly to teach and share this approach. Her dedication and expertise offer a practical, actionable roadmap for using CRAFT techniques to support your loved one.

Through these interviews, I hope you'll see how CRAFT can transform not just your loved one's recovery but also your own sense of hope, confidence, and approach as you navigate this journey. These tools are empowering and will also strengthen your relationship with your loved one as you walk this path together.

This chapter is full of actionable advice and inspiration, so let's get into it.

Jane shared something that I think so many of us can relate to:

"I felt like you get your loved one into treatment, and everything is solved. Things go back to normal, and life is perfect."

But as she worked through the process with her husband, she realized it's not that simple. She learned that conversations about treatment don't just happen once—they happen over time.

"You can't expect to bring it up and have it all work out immediately," she explained.

For Jane, the CRAFT method introduced the idea of looking for "windows of opportunity." These were moments when her husband was more open to conversations about change. She described how these windows would often open after a binge, disappearing from work for days, or feeling deep remorse after an argument.

> "In those moments," she said, "I could plant a seed— make an invitation to get help. One of those windows led to him agreeing to therapy, which eventually opened the door to a treatment facility."

Jane emphasized the importance of acting quickly when those windows open.

> "Once they agree to go, you need to move fast before they change their mind," she said.

Even then, it wasn't always smooth sailing. Her husband had moments where he said he wanted to change but didn't follow through. Other times, he'd agree to treatment but want to leave soon after arriving.

> "It's part of the process," Jane said. "But you have to be ready to act when the moment is right."

She described the challenges her husband faced just getting into treatment. He spent days going through intake, wrestling with the reality of a thirty-day commitment, and worrying about things like activating FMLA, protecting his privacy, and the financial burden.

> "It was a lot for him," she admitted, "but once he started treatment, something shifted. At first, he wanted to go home, but then there came a point where he didn't want to leave ."

Jane said her husband found unexpected peace in the mindfulness practices offered at the treatment facility, things like meditation and tai chi, which helped him manage the stress that had been overwhelming him for years.

"It was a turning point," she said, "but recovery is never linear. I thought we'd be happy right after treatment, but the reality is that the brain needs time to heal."

This was a lesson Jane had to learn along the way.

"I had to reset my expectations," she said. "I thought he'd come out of treatment, and everything would be fine. But there were still hard days, and I had to learn to celebrate the small wins."

She shared how her husband's relapses became fewer and less intense over time.

"If you charted it," she said, "you'd see how the frequency and intensity of his relapses faded. Progress isn't always obvious at first, but it's there."

One thing Jane wished she had done differently was to listen more actively during her husband's struggles.

"He'd tell me how stressful work was, but I wasn't really hearing him," she said. "I just wanted the substance use to stop. Looking back, I wish I had focused more on what he was telling me and tried to address the things that were triggering him."

The CRAFT method helped her realize that improving other areas of her husband's life could reduce his substance use.

"If your loved one says work is stressful, that's a chance to say, 'Let's talk to a career coach.' It opens the door to other conversations, including substance use, and can lead to real change," she said.

Jane also stressed the importance of positive reinforcement.

> "After treatment, I made an effort to focus on communication, active listening, and celebrating his wins. Over time, those small efforts added up. His relapses became less frequent, and eventually, they stopped altogether. I held up a mirror to him, showing him the progress I saw and the potential I knew he had. Eventually, he started to believe it too."

Today, Jane's husband is recovered, and they've built a beautiful life together with their young child. Her experiences inspired her to found We The Village, an organization dedicated to helping families like hers. Jane also partnered with the National Institute on Drug Abuse to further research and understanding around addiction and recovery.

Jane's story is proof that recovery is within reach. It's not linear, and it takes time, patience, and a lot of love. But her journey shows that even the smallest steps forward can lead to meaningful change. Her story is a reminder that no matter how hard things feel, there's always hope.

Hearing Jane say that the brain needs time to heal really struck a chord with me. It's so easy to think that once your loved one comes back from treatment, everything should be right with the world again.

But the truth is, while treatment is such an important piece of the recovery puzzle, it's not everything. There's still work to be done at home, and the tools they're given in treatment are just that—tools. Your loved one needs time, patience, and practice to use them effectively.

Jane's reminder that recovery isn't instant really stayed with me. Knowing this can help us remain patient and supportive, even when things get hard—because they will.

This was such an important point, and one I carry with me. I hope you carry it with you as well—a reminder that change happens over time. We must allow space for healing.

Now that you've heard Jane Mackey's story and her personal experience with the CRAFT method, let's transition into the professional perspective of Michelle Kuecker.

Michelle is a licensed clinical social worker and certified CRAFT trainer who works directly with Dr. Robert Meyers, the founder of the CRAFT method. I had the privilege of interviewing her, and I feel so honored to share her insights with you.

She is not only incredibly knowledgeable, but she's also deeply encouraging. Michelle's practical advice provides a clear roadmap for navigating the challenges you may face with your loved one. I truly believe her guidance will inspire and empower you to take your next steps with both confidence and hope.

According to Michelle, one of the biggest challenges people face when talking to their loved one is saying too much.

> "It's easy to let your emotions take over and start unloading everything you're feeling: 'You're drinking all the time, you're screwing up, we're going to lose the house.' But this approach isn't helpful because your loved one is already thinking the worst. They're far meaner to themselves than you could ever be."

Michelle's advice? Keep it simple, short, and to the point. Focus on what you want from them right now, in that moment.

> "Get to the point of what you need to say without overwhelming your loved one," she said. "It's not about a laundry list of changes but addressing one specific need."

For example, instead of saying:

> "You never come home, you're always at the bar, and I'm tired of this. "

Try:

> "I'm so happy you're home safe. I really worry when I don't hear from you. Can you give me a call next time and just let me know where you are?"

Instead of:

> "You're leaving beer cans everywhere."

Say:

> "It means a lot to me when you clean up after yourself."

Framing your concerns in a positive way and addressing small, specific changes allows you to create space for open communication.

> "Focus on what you want them to do, not what you want them to stop doing," Michelle added. "It makes a world of difference."

Michelle also shared her perspective on recognizing when your loved one might be open to the idea of treatment. She referred to this as the "window of opportunity."

This method involves actively listening to your loved one and identifying moments when they may be more receptive, such as when they vent about stress at work, mention health concerns, or express frustration in the relationship. These are chances to gently extend an invitation to get help.

Michelle suggested responses like:

> "You know, it's been helpful for me to talk to someone when I've felt stressed. I know of this person you could talk to."

She emphasized the importance of preparation.

"Do your homework," she said. "Make calls ahead of time to identify a therapist who specializes in addiction or dual diagnosis. Ensure the therapist knows the full story and that your insurance coverage is in place."

When your loved one agrees to see someone, you typically only have a day or two to act before they might change their mind. A good therapist can take an initial conversation about stress and gently guide it toward the deeper issue of substance use.

"It's all about creating a space where your loved one feels safe and supported," Michelle explained.

Another key point Michelle highlighted was the power of positive reinforcement.

"Your loved one craves positivity," she said. "When you acknowledge the good things they do—like coming home for dinner or spending time with the kids—it helps them feel connected to you, their family, and their community. That connection can reduce their desire to drink."

Examples Michelle gave include:

"The kids love it when you're home for dinner. It means so much to them."

"Thanks for coming home tonight. It made our night."

Michelle likened this to receiving a compliment from your boss:

"It makes you feel good and motivates you to keep up the good work," she said. "Your loved one is no different."

She also explained the importance of addressing "unintentional support"—what many of us traditionally know as enabling.

In CRAFT, we don't use the word 'enabling,'" she explained. "It carries guilt and shame, and that's not productive. Instead, we focus on how to stop unintentional support in ways that feel manageable."

One key tip is to avoid overwhelming your loved one with a laundry list of everything you're no longer willing to do.

Michelle explained that this kind of approach can feel more like a rant than a productive conversation. Instead, focus on one boundary at a time.

For example, instead of saying:

> "I'm done with everything—I'm not buying your alcohol, cleaning up after you, or finding your keys anymore,"

Choose one specific action to address, like not buying alcohol.

When the timing feels right, such as when your loved one is sober and in a good mood, you can say something like:

> "I know I've done this in the past, but I'm not comfortable buying alcohol anymore."

Keep it short, kind, and to the point.

Michelle explained that boundaries can also include smaller actions, like refusing to search for their keys so they can get to the liquor store or declining to clean up their empty beer bottles.

> "It's important to be clear about what you're no longer willing to do," she said, "but it's just as important to praise them when they respect those boundaries. You can't overdo the praise."

Once a boundary is successfully set and respected, you can move on to the next one. Over time, this gradual approach helps build healthier dynamics without overwhelming your loved one or yourself.

When discussing treatment dropouts, Michelle acknowledged how common they are, especially the first time.

> "It's not unusual to get a call saying, 'Get me out of here, I can't do this,'" she said.

Her advice? Buy time. Respond with something like:

> "I hear you, and I know this is hard. Do you think you can make it another hour? Or two hours?"
> "I can't get you tonight, but can we talk about this in the morning?"

During this time, she recommends calling the facility to alert them.

> "Often, a counselor or peer can help talk your loved one through that moment," Michelle said. "It's all about getting through that moment. Every hour they stay is another step forward."

Michelle left me with three key takeaways:

1. Show your love and support by pointing out the positive things your loved one is doing and acknowledging even their smallest efforts.

2. Use positive communication skills to frame tough conversations in a constructive way.

3. Take care of yourself.

> "You can't pour from an empty cup," Michelle reminded. "Self-care is critical."

And finally, she said something I'll never forget:

4. "If all you can remember in the heat of the moment is to show your loved one that you love them and are on their team, that's enough. You're already on the right track. Everything else will fall into place."

Her advice resonated deeply with me, especially when she said that even if the outcome isn't what you hoped for, you can find peace in knowing you've done everything you could to support your loved one with love.

> "You turned over every stone and did it with compassion."

That statement hits home. My outcome with Steve wasn't what I wanted. But I can say, with honesty and peace, that I came from a place of love. I did the work to change myself so I could be there for him, and I gave it my all—with grace and compassion.

Michelle's wisdom is a reminder that this journey is a marathon, not a sprint. It requires patience and, most importantly, coming from a place of love.

Jane's personal story and Michelle's expert advice provide us with so many tools to use and, most importantly, hope.

Let's pull everything together with a few key points you can start implementing right now. These takeaways are designed to give you confidence as you move forward in a positive way with your loved one on this journey.

Michelle's "window of opportunity" method emphasizes listening carefully when your loved one talks about their problems. They might not directly mention their alcohol use, but their concerns often circle back to it.

For example, if your loved one says, "I just haven't been feeling well lately," you might know it's related to substance use. But they may not have made that connection them-selves—or they may not be ready to admit it.

They're focusing on what's bothering them right now: the fact that they don't feel well.

This is your moment to respond with compassion and gently guide them toward help. You could say,

> "I'm sorry you don't feel well. I really want you to feel better. What can I do to help you now? By the way, the doctor I went to when I was having some issues really helped. I'd be happy to have you see him. I think you'll feel better soon. He's a good doctor."

Or if they say, "I just don't have motivation like I used to, but I don't know why," you might respond with:

> "I know someone you could talk to who might be really helpful. Why not just talk to them and see what they think? If it doesn't help, no big deal—but it couldn't hurt to try, right? I can get their number and set it up for you."

This approach works because you're guiding them toward a professional, someone who can uncover the root of their struggles and determine the best path forward, whether that's outpatient or inpatient care.

Your role isn't to fix everything.

Your role is to help them take that first step.

Doing the groundwork—researching therapists, speaking with insurance, and having treatment options ready—sets the stage for progress as soon as your loved one agrees to talk to someone.

What's more, this method changes the tone of your conversations. When you approach your loved one with compassion and understanding, you open the door for meaningful dialogue. You're far more likely to hear a "yes" if you approach with kindness than if you come at them forcefully or confrontationally.

Michelle also emphasized the importance of setting boundaries—but not overwhelming your loved one with a long list of changes.

Imagine how you would feel if someone came at you with a list of everything they wouldn't tolerate anymore. You'd likely feel defensive and shut down emotionally. Your loved one will likely feel the same.

Instead, focus on one manageable boundary at a time. For example, you might say:

> "I know I've done this in the past, but I'm not comfortable buying alcohol for you anymore."

Once you've set that boundary and see your loved one respecting it, follow up with positive reinforcement. Acknowledge their effort, no matter how small. For instance, if your boundary was not cleaning up their empty beer cans, you might praise them for taking responsibility:

> "Thanks for cleaning up. It really helps, and I appreciate it."

Michelle explained that your loved one craves connection. When they feel loved, welcomed, and accepted, they feel closer to you and less isolated. That sense of connection can reduce their desire to drink.

Positive reinforcement helps foster that connection and keeps the lines of communication open.

It bears repeating that you should prepare for the possibility of treatment dropout, which is common, especially during the first attempt. It's not something to fear but something to be aware of. Everyone's journey is different, and the recovery process varies widely in severity and progress.

If your loved one calls and says, "I can't do this," focus on buying time. You might say:

"I hear you, and I know you're struggling right now. Let's just try to get through this hour."

During moments like these, reach out to the treatment facility and collaborate with their staff. Often, a counselor or peer can help your loved one push through that tough moment and stay in treatment.

As Michelle said:

"Every hour they stay is another step forward."

Combining these tools—listening for windows of opportunity, setting manageable boundaries, using positive reinforcement, and being prepared for challenges—sets you and your loved one up for success.

These strategies empower you to play an active and loving role in their recovery.

Don't let yourself feel powerless. These tools are achievable, and they work. There's so much hope in this process, and you've got everything you need to take that next step. Believe in yourself and in the love you have for your loved one.

You can do this.

The common thread in Jane Mackey's story and Michelle Kuecker's expert advice is clear:

Love, compassion, listening, and patience are at the core of recovery.

Jane's story is both relatable and hopeful, beautifully illustrating these principles in action, while Michelle provides the structure and tools needed to navigate the challenges of addiction effectively.

For example, Jane emphasized the importance of slowing down, being realistic about your expectations, and recognizing that by truly listening and approaching the process with patience, you can actually make progress more quickly.

Similarly, Michelle explained that active listening creates windows of opportunity—those pivotal moments when your loved one might be more open to support and a conversation about treatment.

These moments are your chance to gently offer help and guide your loved one toward taking a step forward.

Both perspectives remind us that patience is not just a virtue but a necessity in the journey toward healing. Together, Jane's and Michelle's insights bring this chapter full circle, combining real-life experience with professional expertise. Their shared wisdom offers both hope and actionable steps for you to take.

Recovery is possible. Healing will come. And with love and patience, you can help your loved one find their way forward.

I hope Jane's and Michelle's stories have shown you not only the power of love and compassion but also the power you hold to bring change into even the most difficult situations. The tools provided in this chapter—combined with your consistent support—are a dynamic duo.

You play such an important role in your loved one's healing.

In the next chapter, we'll dive into handling some of the more difficult aspects of addiction, like enabling and manipulation. These behaviors can be hard to recognize and even harder to respond to, but let's take that step together.

Reflection Journal:
Putting CRAFT into Practice
Take a few quiet moments to reflect
and write:

- Did Jane's story or something Michelle shared feel relatable to you, and why?
  (Did it reflect what you're currently experiencing? Did it give you hope?)

- Have you ever missed a "window of opportunity" to talk to your loved one because you panicked, the moment passed, or you were afraid to speak up?
  (What will you do differently next time?)

- What are some boundaries you've been meaning to set but haven't yet?
  (How could you communicate one of those boundaries calmly and confidently?)

- What's one thing from this chapter you want to try in your next conversation?
  (It could be something Michelle said or a CRAFT technique that worked for Jane.)

CHAPTER 11

The Blame Game

When Everything Becomes Your Fault—and What to Do About It

How do you feel when you realize you're being manipulated? Does it make you angry or leave you feeling confused? Manipulation can take many forms. I often think of it as an umbrella with different tactics falling underneath it. Gaslighting, guilt-tripping, and deflecting are some of the most common. These tactics can leave you doubting yourself and questioning your instincts. Recognizing them is the first step to breaking free, and luckily, there are tools you can put into practice.

This is the chapter where we finally begin putting those tools into practice. If you've ever felt uncertain about how to respond during crucial moments or questioned your own sense of reality, you're not alone, and there are things you can say and do that will help restore your confidence.

Gaslighting happens when someone makes you question your memory, perception, or version of events. For example:

> "You're just exaggerating. I only drink a couple of beers at night. There really isn't a problem."

> "My behavior is fine when I drink. It's you that gets all bent out of shape."

These statements are designed to distort your sense of reality and shift the blame onto you.

Guilt-tripping is another tactic where you're made to feel responsible for their behavior. This might sound like:

> "I drink because you stress me out."

> "If you would just let me be, then maybe I'd work on my drinking."

In these cases, the blame for their actions is placed squarely on your shoulders, making you feel at fault for their choices.

Deflecting often involves changing the subject, starting an unrelated argument, or using humor to minimize the issue. For instance, if you try to address their drinking, they might crack a joke to steer the conversation elsewhere or say something completely unrelated to distract you from the topic.

I experienced my fair share of manipulation with Steve, and it came in many different forms. I relied so much on the trust I had built with him that I never questioned his actions. Once I realized his drinking was a problem and tried to bring it up, I felt like Steve used the trust and dynamics of our relationship to his advantage.

Our relationship had always been one where he was the decision-maker, and I was the follower—the one who faithfully believed in his version of what was best. So, when he insisted he didn't have a drinking problem and that he could handle it, I believed him.

The manipulation went on for so long, with statements like:

> "Your stress is causing my stress, and that's why I drink."

> "If you would give me the time and space, maybe I'd make progress, but you're always hovering."

I started to believe these things, and it wasn't until I found myself in a place of physical danger that I finally saw the truth. The manipulation had escalated so much that my home was no longer a safe space. Only then did I fully understand that my feelings had been valid all along. All of it—the gaslighting, guilt-tripping, and deflection—was an attempt to steer me away from seeing the reality of the situation.

Sometimes, when we've been interacting with our loved one the same way for a long period of time, the idea of suddenly drawing a boundary, changing how we communicate, or "opening that can of worms" can feel awkward or even scary.

I felt this deeply with Steve because I had been quiet for so many years, not wanting to rock the boat. I was afraid that if I said something he didn't like or stood up for myself, I would be rejected. That fear of rejection was a big hurdle for me.

Eventually, I came to the realization that I was going to lose him if I didn't stand up for myself. The situation was only going to get worse if nothing changed. But beyond that, I was also losing myself. I wasn't happy. I was sad every day because I allowed myself to be manipulated and let him control every conversation, and now this disease was controlling my life. I felt so lonely in my emotions, and all I wanted was to express them.

One of the best things I did was rehearse what I wanted to say before having those tough conversations—and the responses I knew I'd need when he came back with a manipulation tactic. This was incredibly helpful because it allowed me to gather and organize my thoughts. When we're dealing with so many big emotions and thoughts swirling around in our heads, practicing our responses out loud helps us take control. It gave me the confidence to articulate exactly what I wanted to say and how I wanted to say it.

By practicing, I was able to come across as confident and sure of myself. My words were clear and purposeful, and the message I delivered was both meaningful and productive.

Once you recognize these tactics, you can then learn how to respond in ways that are productive. The goal isn't to point fingers or argue; it's to draw a line where your boundaries are and stop the cycle of manipulation.

Let's look at some examples of how gaslighting, guilt-tripping, and deflection often show up—and how you can respond in a way that leaves you feeling confident and in control.

Gaslighting

When they say:

> "You're being dramatic. I really don't have a problem."

Expanded Example:

You bring up concerns about their drinking, and instead of acknowledging anything, they deny it. Suddenly, you're questioning who's right. Was I overreacting? Did I misinterpret what happened? Maybe it really isn't as bad as it seems.

Try saying:

> "I'm not trying to make you feel guilty or attack you. I'm sharing how I feel and what I see. I've noticed changes that concern me, and I should be able to talk to you about that. My facts might not always be perfect, but my feelings are valid, even if we don't agree."

Why this works:

You're not debating whether or not they have a problem. You're holding your ground on your feelings, and feelings are harder to argue with or invalidate.

Guilt-Tripping

When they say:

> "I drink because you stress me out. If you didn't nag me all the time, maybe I'd be better."

Expanded Example:

This one stings, especially if you already feel guilty for bringing it up again. It makes you question whether your concern is the cause of their drinking, and suddenly, you're the one apologizing.

Try saying:

> "I understand that you're stressed, and I think you have valid reasons to feel that way. That's not what I want for either of us. But how you choose to deal with stress—whether that's drinking or something else—is still your choice. There are healthier ways to cope, and I believe you're capable of finding them."

Why this works:

It acknowledges their feelings without accepting the blame. You keep the door open for connection but don't allow the manipulation to stick.

Deflection

When they say:

> "You always want to talk about this when I'm trying to relax. Just drop it."

Expanded Example:

Suddenly, you're arguing about timing instead of discussing the real issue. Now you're defending why you brought it up, and the original concern gets buried.

Try saying:

"I'm not here to fight. I just want to talk about something important to me. I'm open to a better time, so let's pick one together today."

Why this works:

You're showing flexibility and respect, but you're not backing down. You're reinforcing that your concerns matter while reducing the chance of escalation.

These responses allow you to be assertive without causing an argument. They show that you're coming from a place of love and concern rather than trying to control the situation.

Responding with confidence may take some practice, but it's something you'll grow comfortable with quickly. Once you rip off that Band-Aid, so to speak, you'll likely feel an immediate sense of relief. Expressing yourself in a matter-of-fact, calm, and concise way is incredibly empowering.

The best way to prepare is to practice these responses ahead of time, either by yourself or with someone you trust. Practicing gives you the space to gather your thoughts and stay grounded, so when the moment comes, you're ready to speak clearly and confidently.

Boundaries are essential to protecting your emotional well-being. They give you the ability to feel heard and understood while fostering mutual respect in your relationship. Setting boundaries isn't about asserting control or regaining power; it's about creating space for healthy communication so that better choices can be made.

One of the most effective ways to communicate boundaries is by starting with "I" statements. Starting with "I" keeps the focus on your feelings and observations, rather than accusing or blaming the other person. It's a way of saying "This is how I feel and what I need" without putting the other person on the defensive.

Other Examples of Setting Boundaries

Let's explore how to set boundaries in response to common manipulation tactics.

Gaslighting Example

> Steve might say:
> "I was released from the hospital, so I'm fine. My medical issues aren't serious. You just like to make things dramatic "

Response:
> "I understand why you'd feel that way, but I need you to take my concerns seriously. It's not okay to dismiss my feelings."

Guilt-Tripping Example

> "We had a bad weekend because you nagged me about my drinking."

Response:
> "I understand your frustration, but I'm not responsible for your choices. I voiced my concern because I care about your health, and I want to support you."

Deflection Example

They bring up unrelated topics or try to turn the conversation back on you.

Response:
> "I understand your frustration, and I'm happy to discuss how I can improve after we finish this conversation. Right now, I'd like to stick to this topic because it's important to me."

Boundaries can be tough to set, especially when you haven't enforced them before. It can feel scary and intimidating, particularly if you have the same fears I had, like the fear of rejection. But that's why role-playing is such a helpful tool. I know it might sound silly at first, but I promise this practice can make all the difference.

Take a few minutes—whether it's in your car, in the shower, or somewhere quiet where you can gather your thoughts—and practice speaking out loud. You're going to fine-tune exactly what you want to say. And don't worry, it doesn't have to be perfect. It might not come out exactly as you rehearsed, and that's okay.

Another reason rehearsing your words is so valuable is that it helps you prepare for the pushback you'll likely receive. Practicing your responses means you can anticipate those moments and stay in control when they happen.

Here's how to break it down into steps:

Step 1: Choose a Recurring Scenario

Think of a situation you often encounter with your loved one—something they say or do repeatedly. Pick one specific behavior or comment you want to address. Focus on just one point, keeping it brief and to the point to maintain their attention.

Examples:

- *Gaslighting*:
  "I really feel like you're dismissing my feelings when you tell me this is all in my head. My feelings are valid, and I need you to take me seriously when I express them."

- *Guilt-Tripping*:
  "I understand this is hard for you, and I truly sympathize

with your side of it. But I'm not responsible for your re-actions, and I need you to know my words come from a place of love."

- *Deflection:*
"I understand that you don't want to talk about this right now, and I've tried to put myself in your shoes. I know I'd feel the same way. But this is important to me, and I need us to hear each other out."

Step 2: Practice Out Loud

Once you've chosen your scenario and crafted your response, say it out loud.

These are just examples; phrase things in a way that feels natural to you and fits your specific situation. You can even journal your responses to refine them further and have them as a reference.

The goal isn't perfection. It's about getting comfortable voicing your feelings and setting those boundaries aloud. This practice will help you find your confidence and stay composed, even in the face of pushback.

Step 3: Anticipate Pushback

Be prepared for potential resistance. Your loved one might dismiss your feelings, say they don't care, or even walk away mid-conversation. That's okay. The more you assert yourself, the more their negative responses will diminish over time. They'll begin to understand what you will and won't tolerate.

Step 4: Visualize the Outcome

Take a moment to close your eyes and picture the scenario playing out. Visualize yourself remaining calm, composed, and confident. Imagine how good it will feel to express yourself clearly and stay in control of the conversation. This visualization reinforces your ability to follow through with these new habits and helps create a positive mindset.

The more you practice, the better you'll get at staying calm and assertive during real-life conversations. This is a new habit, and it might feel awkward at first, but stick with it. You'll start to see shifts in the dynamic of your relationship—shifts that lead to healthier communication and more positive changes overall.

You can do this. Trust the process, take it one step at a time, and know that every time you practice, you're building a stronger foundation for yourself and your relationship.

We know that boundaries are important to your emotional well-being, but do you understand why your boundaries help your loved one heal?

If you don't set boundaries, your loved one has nothing to reflect on. They're sent the message that their behavior is okay—that it's perfectly acceptable to carry on as they are and that they don't need to change.

They need to be given something to reflect on—not all at once but one thing at a time to work on and improve.

You want them to reflect and take accountability for their actions, for how they made you and others around them feel, and for the things they have done or said. You can do this by using the tools you've been given and doing so in a way that removes the judgment. Both of you will feel respected.

Showing your loved one that respect will be given and that it goes both ways allows you to build a stronger, more balanced relationship.

We talked about how rehearsing your words and taking it a step further by role-playing with someone you trust builds confidence and how quickly you can start to see changes once you begin using it in response to manipulation tactics. The same principle applies to setting boundaries. Practicing how you respond works in all real-life situations, not just this one. It's a valuable life tool to incorporate into your daily routine.

If there's a boundary you've been avoiding, it's time to face it.

For example, maybe you no longer want to:

- Supply alcohol.
- Clean up after empty beer cans.
- Cover up when your loved one experiences the natural consequences of their substance use.

These boundaries are hard to set—I get it. Confrontation can be scary. But think about the alternative.

What are you gaining by not setting that boundary?
Are you gaining respect?
Or are you holding on to hope that things will change, even though they haven't?

Hope alone is not a strategy.

Without a strategy, change is unlikely to happen. You have the power to be the driving force for change, not just for yourself but also for your loved one. By setting and enforcing boundaries, you transform your own life during this journey, and in doing so, you create the space for your loved one to heal as well.

You can be the spark that ignites the change you want to see in this journey. Remember, while you can only control yourself, you absolutely have the power to inspire. And that is what you'll begin to see happen as you take these steps.

I know it isn't easy to recognize manipulation, let alone decide you're going to speak up and set boundaries. This is a tough thing at first.

But I repeat: at first.

Throughout my journey, I transformed in ways I never thought I would or could—and you will too. That change doesn't happen overnight, and I didn't notice it as it was happening. But one day, I found myself saying, "Wow, who is this girl who speaks up for herself confidently?" You will have that moment, too. I know you will.

As you stand up for yourself and your relationship, you're building a healthy foundation. It's hard work, but it's worth it. This is about seeing progress, not about being perfect or overthinking what to say.

Every time you use these tools, you're becoming stronger. You're on your way now!

Keep putting into practice all the tools you've learned so far, and remember:

Thoughts become things.

Mindset matters.

Your effort will move you forward to that future you want for yourself and your loved one.

Quick Recap: What You Can Start Using Today

- ✓ Recognize manipulation tactics like gaslighting, guilt-tripping, and deflection.

- ✓ Respond with confident, loving phrases that shift the dynamic.

- ✓ Set and communicate one boundary at a time using "I" statements.

- ✓ Use role-playing or journaling to rehearse hard conversations in advance.

- ✓ Visualize staying calm, collected, and in control.

✓ Remember, your boundaries—and staying firm—give
them something to reflect on.

Every one of these tools helps you shift the energy. You're
no longer reacting—you're leading with strength and clarity.
This is not easy at first—but I repeat: at first. You won't always
see your growth while it's happening, but it is happening.
I'd compare it to watching your children grow. One minute
they're crawling, and the next they're walking. With every
boundary you set, every time you speak up, and every time
you stay grounded in your truth, you're moving forward. Even
the smallest changes are signs of real progress.

Every time you choose to respond differently, you're dis-
rupting the old pattern. That's what creates momentum—not
by controlling the other person but by leading with clarity
and strength.

Eventually, I found myself saying, "Wow, I've really
changed so much. I'm confident, I advocate for myself, and
look—I've learned so much that I'm writing this book for others now."

That will be you one day.

My mom once told me something that stuck with me,
and I still use it today. She said, "Choose your hard." She's
been saying it since I was a kid. What she meant was this:
every decision is tough. Loving someone with an addiction is
hard. Walking away is hard. Finding your voice and learning
the tools to get through this is hard. But doing nothing and
watching the fallout? That's hard too. So, choose your hard.
The hard work is worth it.

This is about seeing the progress—not getting every single word right. It's about letting go of the pressure to say everything just right. Every time you use these tools, you'll feel

more confident. You're on your way now! Keep putting them into practice. And remember, thoughts become things, mind-set matters, and your effort will carry you toward the future you want—for yourself and for your loved one.

You are not alone in this. With every word you speak from a place of clarity and love, you're redirecting your course—and theirs.

In the next chapter, we'll explore how to handle resistance when it arises—because it will. Together, we'll navigate these challenges with love and understanding, giving you all the tools you need to keep pushing forward.

Reflection Journal: Responding to Manipulation and Setting Boundaries

Take a few quiet moments to reflect and write:

- If you're experiencing manipulation, which tactic shows up most often in your relationship—gaslighting, guilt-tripping, or deflection?
  (How do you typically feel in that moment?)

- Think back to the last time you felt manipulated. If you could go back, how would you respond differently?
  (Try writing it out now, as if you're speaking in this moment, with calm and confidence.)

- What's one frequently recurring scenario that you want to practice responding to?
  (Picture it clearly. What do you want to say? How do you want to feel afterward?)

CHAPTER 12

Handling Resistance with Calm, Care, and Confidence

Resistance to change is natural in any journey. It's especially common when you're talking about changing addictive behaviors or asking someone to seek help to overcome their addiction. You might hear statements from your loved one such as, "I don't need help," or "I don't have a problem." When you hear things like this—things you know aren't true—it's easy to get angry. But anger closes the conversation and the door to progress. Remaining calm is the only way to keep that door open.

For example, a typical response when talking about seeking help might be:

> Them: "I'm too busy. I just don't want to talk about this right now."

> You: "I understand that now is not a good time.

> How about if we just schedule an appointment with your doctor and start with something small that they suggest? How does that sound?"

> Or, if you hear:

"I've tried to quit, and I just can't. It's just not what I want to do right now," you could say,

"I understand why it would be difficult, and if it's helping you, then it's completely understandable that you don't want to quit. I do worry about your health, though. Let's just go talk with someone who can help provide some suggestions. What do you think?"

These types of responses validate their feelings while offering steps that feel doable. They show your loved one that you understand them, that you care, and that you're willing to work with them rather than control or overwhelm them.

Imagine your loved one saying:
"When things get stressful in the house, I like to have a drink."
You could respond with:
"I understand that things get stressful, and I can relate to that. I do notice that in the moment, it relaxes you, but later, you don't feel well, and it's affecting you in negative ways. I care about you. How do you feel about that?"

This kind of response makes them feel heard and understood without condoning the behavior or encouraging it to continue. Instead, you're gently pointing out that what makes them feel good in the short term also has consequences. Keeping calm during the conversation and staying on point can help them begin to reflect on their behavior.

This chapter will give you the tools you need to feel better equipped when facing resistance. You'll learn how to handle these situations appropriately while staying calm, and by the end of this chapter, you'll feel confident and ready to try these strategies so you can keep moving forward.

Before we get into the tools and strategies I'll be teaching, I want you to understand why resistance happens—and how you can approach it more effectively. When you understand what's behind the resistance, you're able to respond with empathy. And that empathy will be genuine when you really understand your loved one.

I'm ashamed to admit that I reached a point with Steve where I was so frustrated by his resistance, especially when it came to staying in treatment for the recommended length of time or agreeing to go back. I was at my wits' end and resorted to yelling and threatening him, but it didn't work. I wasn't taking the time to understand why he was so resistant. I was only focused on wanting a quick solution.

Eventually, I stopped and really thought about the why behind his resistance. I finally heard what he had been trying to tell me all along: he was scared. Once I realized that, I was able to change my tone and speak to the fear underneath his resistance. It shifted our conversations completely. That change built trust, and that trust opened the door to deeper conversations and his willingness to consider change and new possibilities.

Keep in mind that while understanding is key to empathy, empathy alone isn't enough. You also need tools to help you stay calm during those intense, tough moments—and I want to share one of the most effective ones with you next.

Be prepared. Conversations about quitting substance use or seeking treatment can get intense. It's easy to let your emotions take over. You're trying to help, but when your loved one resists, it can feel hopeless—like there's nowhere to turn.

In these moments, I want you to stay calm. Staying calm is critical. If you yell or have an emotional outburst, the conversation will likely end abruptly and not in a productive way. Worse—your loved one may be less open the next time. Keeping the dialogue going is key.

One thing I found incredibly helpful is a tool called the STOP Method. It's a simple, practical technique that teaches you how to pause, recenter yourself, and return to the conversation grounded, calm, and empathetic, just as you had planned. The more you practice it, the more natural it becomes. Here's how it works:

S – Stop
When you feel your face getting hot, your voice tightening, or your emotions bubbling to the surface, pause the conversation. It's helpful to have a code word with your loved one so they understand you're taking a short break, which I'll explain shortly. Then, go silent for a few moments.

T – Take a Deep Breath
Close your eyes and inhale deeply. Deep breathing slows your heart rate and calms your nervous system.

O – Observe
Check in with yourself. Ask, How am I feeling? Am I calm enough to continue? Observe your body language, your tone, and your posture. If you're still tense, pause a little longer.

P – Proceed
Once you feel calm and composed, let your loved one know that you're ready to continue. You're now in a

place where your words and energy are more aligned with your intention—to connect, not to escalate.

I remember so many conversations with Steve where I poured my heart out, begging him to stop drinking. When he deflected, I often broke down. I would melt into tears, crying uncontrollably until I was so emotionally drained that we couldn't pick the conversation back up that day.

In those moments, I let my emotions take control, and it completely shut me down. I was exhausted, defeated, and too spent to keep going.

That's why this tool matters. The STOP method won't just help you stay in the conversation—it will help you preserve your energy, maintain your boundaries, and keep the door open for meaningful change.

Taking this step shows your loved one that you're committed to approaching conversations in a calm, thoughtful way, and it's something they will likely appreciate.

Now that you have a good understanding of why this resistance occurs, let's focus on what steps you can take to help your loved one progress. This next set of tools will help you to open communication and dialogue, something that is a common struggle.

Looking back, I see how, in those moments, he had "won" the battle, not because he was right but because the conversation had gone nowhere. This happened so many times, and each time left me feeling more defeated.

When I began to implement the tools I'm teaching you now, everything changed. I started coming to conversations with a plan and a clear purpose. I practiced deep breathing to regulate my emotions and allowed myself time to pause before reacting. When Steve resisted or deflected and the

conversation didn't go as planned, I stayed calm and grounded because I had responses ready. I didn't lose myself in the
moment anymore.

These tools gave me a sense of confidence I didn't have.
Even when progress was slow, I knew I was showing up to
these conversations with purpose, and I could see the dynamic starting to change.

The STOP method might feel awkward at first, but over
time, it will become something you won't want to be without.
It's helpful to explain this technique to your loved one ahead
of time so that when you pause during a conversation, they
don't become frustrated or confused. You can say something
like, "Hey, I know I can get emotional or worked up sometimes when we're talking, and I'm really working on that. If I
say STOP—or another code word—it's not because I'm mad
at you. I just need a minute to take a deep breath and pause
because this really helps me."

Now, I want you to take a moment to actually practice
this method. Close your eyes and picture a conversation that
keeps coming up—one that often gets your emotions boiling.
Imagine yourself pausing, saying "STOP," and taking a deep
breath. Then, visualize yourself continuing the conversation
calmly and with confidence. Practicing this now will help you
feel more prepared and self-assured when you put it into action with your loved one.

Now that you've learned how to stay calm and composed
during challenging conversations, let's focus on techniques
to keep those conversations moving forward productively.
These tools are designed to gently open the door when discussing quitting substance use or seeking treatment, to reduce defensiveness, and to take steps toward change.

For your loved one, even the smallest steps forward can feel overwhelming—and that's completely understandable, not just for someone struggling with addiction but for anyone facing a mental health challenge. They may be just coming to terms with the realization that they have a problem, or perhaps they aren't fully aware of it yet. On top of that, they're already dealing with emotional, mental, and possibly physical consequences. When you think about it, expecting them not to feel overwhelmed by the idea of fixing everything at once is simply not realistic.

This is where guidance becomes essential. Breaking the process into small, manageable steps can make all the difference. Helping your loved one take it one step at a time shows them that progress is doable without tackling everything at once. Let's explore some practical ways to approach these changes in a way that feels more achievable.

One of the most effective ways to keep a conversation moving is not just by remaining calm but by using positive reinforcement, acknowledging even the smallest effort. This could mean recognizing their willingness to sit down and discuss their substance use, agreeing to talk to someone, or any action that signals they're opening up. Whatever the effort may be, it needs to be acknowledged.

For example:

If they simply admit they're struggling with substance abuse, you could say, "I'm so proud of you for saying that out loud. It takes a lot of courage to recognize that and to share it. I know that's not easy."

If they mention feeling down, depressed, or struggling in another area of life without directly referencing substance use, you might respond with:

"I'm sorry you're struggling. I'm really glad you feel comfortable sharing your feelings with me. Just recognizing that you don't feel like yourself is such an important first step."

Sometimes, expressing feelings indirectly—without naming the substance use—is still an acknowledgment of the issue, the elephant in the room. What matters most is that they're communicating their emotions, and that alone is progress worth recognizing.

Any first step, big or small, is worth celebrating. Whether it's cutting back on substance use, agreeing to explore treatment, or simply sitting down for a conversation, these are all steps forward. It's a broad spectrum of progress, but it's all progress—and that's the point.

When you acknowledge your loved one's effort, no matter how small, it builds trust and shows them they're not alone in this. In turn, they'll feel less resistant and more open to continuing the journey.

Positive reinforcement helps to get your loved one to open up and lower their defenses, but what do you do when they actually start to share their struggles?

Reflective listening is the next step. This technique helps your loved one feel truly heard and understood in their feelings and struggles. It's not about solving the problem for them. It's about validating their emotions. When you do this, you lower defensiveness and resistance, which keeps the conversation moving forward in a productive way.

Let's look at how this can play out in a conversation:

- If your loved one says, "I can't quit drinking. I just can't do it because it's too hard... "

  You can validate their feelings by saying:

"I hear you. It sounds like the thought of quitting or even cutting back is really scary, and you're not sure how to move forward."

- If they say, "I know I have a problem with drinking, but I'm not ready to do anything about it yet. I need you to let me figure this out... "

  You can respond with:

  "I hear that you need to feel comfortable with how you move forward. Change can be scary, and I do understand that."

- Or if they say, "I feel like I screw up all the time... "

  You can respond with:

  "It sounds like things are really overwhelming for you right now, and you feel like your efforts aren't paying off. I've felt like that before, too, and I get it."

This method works for a number of reasons. Reflecting their concerns back to them shows that you were really listening and that you understand where they're coming from. It also encourages them to think more deeply about what they just said and consider it further. Taking the judgment out of the equation makes it so you're opening up the conversation and encouraging deeper, more meaningful dialogue.

So, you've lowered their defenses, and you have their attention. This is good. Let's keep the momentum going by asking open-ended questions. When faced with resistance to reducing substance use or understanding why your loved one isn't willing to consider treatment, it's essential to uncover the "why" behind their feelings and responses. Open-ended questions are the key to getting there.

Starting with open-ended questions is great. It accomplishes the goal of getting your loved one to reflect on their choices, ponder their fears, and verbalize what's holding them back. But motivational interviewing takes this a step further. It doesn't just invite reflection—it steers your loved one toward exploring change.

Motivational interviewing acts as a mirror. When you ask open-ended questions and use reflective listening, you're mirroring back not just the words they say to you but the emotions and deeper meanings behind those words. This technique helps them connect the dots, showing how their current behaviors might not align with the life they want. The goal is to guide them gently toward the direction they truly want to go.

Let's look at some practical examples of how to use motivational interviewing in real conversations.

Scenario 1: Cutting Down on Drinking
You ask your loved one, "What do you think about cutting down on drinking?"
They respond:
"Cutting down is really hard. I try, but it helps with my anxiety and takes the edge off, so I don't think I can do it."
You might reflect their feelings and gently guide the conversation with:
"It sounds like you're doing what you can to cope, and drinking feels like a way to manage that stress. What would it feel like if you had other tools to handle anxiety—things that didn't make you feel worse later?"

Scenario 2: Suggesting Treatment
You say: "Would you ever consider talking to someone or going to treatment?"

They respond:

"I don't need treatment. I can handle this on my own."

Try responding with:

"I hear that. It sounds like you want to be in control of the process, and I respect that. What if we just talked to someone to get some options? No pressure to commit to anything, just gathering information."

Scenario 3: Avoiding the Conversation

You try to bring up their drinking, and they say:

"I don't want to talk about this again. You're always on my case."

Instead of backing down or getting defensive, you might say:

"I can see how it might feel that way, and that's not what I want. I just care about you, and I want us to be able to talk openly. What would make these conversations feel more comfortable for you?"

Here's how you can start using this technique.

Start with a question that encourages them to reflect. It can be about whether their substance use is a problem, why they're hesitant to seek help, or whether cutting back might be worth considering. Here's how it could look:

"What do you think about the idea of cutting down on your drinking or going to treatment?"

"What makes this feel like the right decision, and what about it feels like it's not the right thing for you?"

These questions get your loved one to weigh the pros and cons, verbalizing their hesitation while also exploring potential benefits.

You can also say:

"Tell me how drinking makes you feel."

After their response, you can follow up with:

"I'd like to understand more about what it does for you emotionally and physically. I know you feel like it helps you. Can you also share how you think it might hurt you or make you feel worse sometimes? What's that like in those moments?"

This approach gets them to consider not just what they think they're gaining but also the drawbacks of their substance use.

Additionally:

"How do you think your drinking affects aspects of your life, like relationships, work, or your health?"

"Do you think there's an impact?"

Asking these questions in succession helps them see potential consequences they might not typically acknowledge.

Also:

"If things stay the same and you continue drinking, what do you see the future looking like?"

"Do you think things will improve or stay the same? How about your health or relationships—what do you think those will look like?"

These consecutive questions encourage them to think about the consequences of continuing on their current path.

You can even continue with the following train of thought:

"Hypothetically, if you went to treatment or decided to cut back on drinking, how do you think your relationships, health, or performance at work would improve?

Or:

"How do you imagine daily life might feel if you woke up every morning without the desire or need to drink? What would that be like?"

These sets of questions help them envision what life without alcohol could look like, including solutions to some of the negative consequences they may currently be facing.

Here's how you can take this even further:

"On a scale of one to ten, how important is it for you to make a change?"

"What do you feel you need to make that happen?" This is a simple and non-threatening way to gauge where they are in their willingness to change and uncover any barriers they might need help addressing.

And this is how treatment gets brought up in a non-confrontational way after you've arrived this deep in the conversation:

"If you were to decide today to cut back on drinking or agree to get help, what would the next step look like?"

"What would you need to make that step possible?"

Or:

"What's the most difficult part about saying yes to getting help? What do you feel holds you back, and how can we work together to help you feel ready for that step?"

Once you've asked these open-ended questions and started getting responses, the next step is to let your loved one know they've been heard. Reflective listening is key. It validates their feelings and encourages them to keep sharing.

For example, your loved might say:

"I know I need to cut back on drinking, but it's so hard."

You might respond with:

"I hear you. It's hard, and I can only imagine how consuming it must feel to think about cutting back, even though it's important to you."

Next, reinforce their capabilities and strengths by saying something like:

You're being so honest about how difficult this is. That takes a lot of guts."

From there, ask follow-up questions to dig deeper into their feelings and barriers:

"I know you're overwhelmed. What part of agreeing to get help feels the most difficult for you? Why do you think that is?"

"You've said you're not ready to make changes. What do you think you need in order to feel ready?"

Identifying gaps between their current behavior and their goals is especially helpful. This isn't about making them feel guilty; it's about helping them see how their behaviors might not align with their desires.

For example:

"You've told me you want to spend more quality time with us as a family and really be present, but you've also said drinking helps you. How do you think drinking is affecting your ability to commit to that?"

"You've mentioned wanting to improve your health and that you know you can't continue drinking and be healthy. How do you see yourself achieving your health goals while continuing to drink?"

When your loved one shares their thoughts, it's important to summarize what they've said. This shows them you've been listening actively and gives them a chance to hear their own words reflected back, which can encourage further clarity and reflection.

For example:
"So, what I'm hearing is that you really want to improve your health and value our family relationship, but quitting feels overwhelming and scary. You're unsure how to take the next step —is that right?"

Once you've reflected and summarized, you can help them start thinking about next steps. This might involve walking them through what taking those steps could look like, but always make it clear that the ultimate choice is theirs. Respecting their autonomy is crucial. It builds trust and keeps the dialogue open.

You can say something like:
"I know this is your decision, and I want to support you unconditionally. I'm here for you no matter what you choose."

By respecting their choices, you maintain their trust while gently steering them toward the help they need. Trust is essential. If they feel pressured or judged, you risk losing the progress you've made.

We've talked about how change doesn't happen overnight. It takes time and often builds through small, manageable steps. These smaller steps make change less intimidating and more achievable. Each one allows your loved one to look back and see their progress or gain the confidence to take another, larger step.

Alcoholism exists on a spectrum. For some, entering treatment might feel overwhelming and too big of a leap. For others, quitting drinking with some support might seem possible, but even that feels daunting. Taking those big steps—whether quitting drinking or entering treatment—can often start with smaller, more manageable actions.

For example, it could begin with going to a group meeting, cutting back on drinking, talking to their doctor, or meeting with a counselor. These are all meaningful steps forward.

> You can encourage these actions by saying something like:
>
> "What if you started by going to a group meeting? It might be nice to talk with someone who's been through this too."
>
> Or:
>
> "Your doctor might have some good suggestions if you're not ready to commit to treatment yet. Let's find out what options are available."

Since we know small steps make the difference, imagine if your loved one agrees to attend a group meeting or meet with a counselor to discuss treatment options. When they take this step, you can respond with positive reinforcement by saying something like:

"I'm so glad you're doing this. I know it's not easy to talk about, but I can see that you want to try something new, and the fact that you're willing is huge."

Letting your loved one know they are making the right decision—that just the willingness to try matters—is what gets you closer to that bigger goal.

When your loved one takes a step, no matter how small, acknowledge their effort and celebrate it.

For example, if they agree to attend a meeting or talk to a counselor, you might say:

"I'm so proud of you for taking this step. It's a big deal, and I know how hard it was for you. You should be proud of yourself, too."

Recognizing and celebrating their progress builds their confidence, making it easier for them to move toward the next step. Often, one small action naturally leads to another.

For instance, if your loved one begins attending meetings like AA, they may hear from peers that additional support—like treatment—could benefit them. Hearing this from someone who shares their struggle—someone who understands—can often resonate more than hearing it from you.

You can also explore low-pressure options together from the comfort of home.

For example, you could set up a virtual meeting with a doctor or counselor or join a Facebook support group together. Even watching an inspiring story online can spark reflection. You might say:

"I came across this video of someone sharing how they quit drinking. They talked about the steps they took, and it seemed so doable. Want to watch it together?"

These small steps naturally lead to big changes. By supporting your loved one through these steps, you're showing them they can achieve what they didn't think they could.

The tools in this chapter—staying calm, building empathy, and using strategies like positive reinforcement and motivational interviewing—work together to create small wins that build on one another. With these tools in your toolbox, you're well-equipped to approach resistance and guide your loved one toward meaningful change.

Now, with all of these tools in your toolbox, you're ready to guide your loved one.

Another way to keep conversations open when discussing the problem or the possibility of entering treatment is to use "I" statements. We already know these topics can be intense and that conversations can shut down quickly. To reduce defensiveness, "I" statements can be an effective method to keep the dialogue going longer.

"I" statements allow you to express what you're feeling without pointing the finger.

They help you get your message across without the other person feeling like they're being attacked. Let me show you what I mean:

For example, instead of saying,

"You're drinking so much, you're driving us into bankruptcy," you could say,

"I feel scared when I see that we're struggling financially, and it's causing me a lot of anxiety."

Or instead of saying,

You're drunk all the time, and you don't spend time with us," you could say,

I feel hurt and lonely when I feel like we're not spending enough time together as a family. I enjoy being with you, and I want that time with you."

Phrasing it like this makes what you're saying about you and your feelings. You're sharing how their behavior impacts you, rather than accusing them of doing something wrong. In turn, this approach makes it more likely for them to truly listen and consider what you're saying.

Take the "I" statements a step further and ask a follow-up question. For example, after expressing your feelings about wanting to spend more time together, you could ask an open-ended question like:

"What do you think is holding us back from spending more quality time together?"

This allows time and space for that person to ponder whether they might have anything to do with the reason why you aren't—and if drinking comes into play. They already know the answer, but without these follow-up questions, they likely aren't thinking about it.

These questions often prompt an honest response, and that's your opportunity for positive reinforcement, which then encourages change. Combining "I" statements with these follow-up questions really forces that self-reflection, which in turn nudges them toward that next step. It's a natural progression.

The next step in guiding this process is to plant those seeds of hope. Help your loved one see that the big changes they feel are out of reach are actually within their grasp. Many people experiencing ongoing struggles feel isolated, as if they're the only ones dealing with this challenge. While this isn't true, it's a common and normal feeling. By pointing out that they're not alone—and sharing a story of hope from someone who has recovered—you can help break that isolation.

You might share an inspirational quote or find someone on social media who has shared their journey. Bring it up casually, saying something like,

> "This popped up on my Instagram today. This person shares their journey, and I went through their posts. They show how they started with small steps, and now they're doing so well. They even talk about how they got there. What they're sharing seems really doable, and it made me think of you."

When having conversations about change or taking steps forward, remind yourself—and your loved one—that big change often starts small. Almost always, in fact. Highlight their capabilities and the progress they've already made. You might say:

> "Look at what you've already done. Look at the accomplishments you've made so far. That's amazing, and I know you can do even more."

It's also important to prepare for pushback. Resistance doesn't mean failure—it's just part of the process. Let your loved one know that not being ready for big changes yet is okay. Even small steps are meaningful strides. Remind them—and yourself—that these are not failures. They are huge victories.

When you're met with pushback, maintain your empathetic tone. Don't meet resistance with frustration; meet it with understanding. For example, if your loved one says,

"I'm not ready to make a big change,"
you could respond with:
"I hear you. It sounds like a big change feels overwhelming right now, and that's okay. I'm here to support you no matter what steps you feel ready to take."

As you continue having these conversations, remember that it's not just about the big milestones. The small steps are where real momentum begins.

Finally, don't forget to celebrate the small wins. Whether it's agreeing to talk to someone, going to one meeting, or simply opening up about their feelings, these moments matter. Acknowledge their progress with enthusiasm and encouragement. For example:

"I'm so proud of the steps you're taking. Your drive is inspiring."

This chapter has given you tools to handle resistance with love, empathy, and purpose. Resistance is almost guaranteed, but when you're prepared, you can approach it calmly and effectively. It can feel overwhelming and stressful, but with these methods, you're taking real steps forward, opening your loved one up to deeper conversations and gradually breaking through the resistance.

Now that we've explored how to handle resistance by staying calm, using positive reinforcement, asking open-ended questions, and communicating with "I" statements, do you see how these tools work together to break down that wall?

I need you to remember: you're not going to fix everything overnight. But even the smallest steps add up to real progress, and that's what creates lasting change. Every conversation, every interaction, is an opportunity for growth.

So, take a moment to picture that next conversation. Which tool do you want to start with? Motivational interviewing? An "I" statement? It doesn't have to be perfect. What matters is that you begin. That first step will lead to the next.

In the next chapter, we'll talk about expectations, what it means to set realistic ones, and how to navigate the differences between yours and your loved one's. This can be one of the most challenging parts of the journey. How do you come together when you're not on the same page? Let's dive in and talk about how to work through those differences and move forward together as a team.

CHAPTER 13

When Wake-Up Calls
Aren't Realizations

When Steve finally woke up after spending three months in a coma, I had been right there, holding vigil every day. That stretch in the ICU felt like the longest period of my life, and I truly believed that when he opened his eyes and became coherent again, everything would change. He had gone into liver and kidney failure, and although he would ultimately pass away from this disease, this time—somehow—he survived. This happened months before he had gone into inpatient treatment.

His body had been through so much trauma. He had lost all his muscle and had to relearn how to walk. He had a trach, so he had to work on speaking and eating again. On top of all that, he was completely disoriented. He didn't remember anything about what had happened. The doctors explained to me that, while I was fully aware of how close he came to dying, Steve had no memory of it. In his mind, he had simply walked into the hospital and then woken up from a three-month-long nap.

Without any memory of what happened—or any witness to the trauma he endured—there was no realization for him.

He couldn't connect his actions to his near-death experience. For me, this was a devastating reality. I was so sure that this would be his wake-up call, but for him, it wasn't.

The focus during this time wasn't on his drinking or going to rehab; it was on his physical recovery. He went to a rehab center to regain his strength and mobility, and I couldn't even bring up treatment for his addiction yet. That had to wait, which was incredibly frustrating.

When he finally came home, I thought being back with his family might be what he needed to realize how close we had come to losing him.

I watched him work so hard in physical therapy. I kept thinking, "Great! He's going to get in shape—maybe even get hot again." Turns out, he wasn't training for recovery. He was training so he could get in the car and drive himself to the liquor store.

It didn't take long for him to fall back into his old habit of drinking a half gallon a day.

Managing Expectations Without Losing Hope

At this point, we hadn't even talked about treatment—not seriously, anyway. That was when I tried to have the conversation about getting help. I was ready to talk about treatment, but Steve wasn't. To me, this was the logical next step, but for him, it felt like it came out of nowhere. While I had spent months processing and preparing for this, nothing about his perspective had changed.

That disconnect—the gap between what I expected and where he was—was one of the hardest things to face. I had expected him to connect the dots, to realize the consequences of his actions, and make a change. But he didn't see it that way.

Do you ever wonder why they can't just quit drinking? You both know there's a problem, but they keep picking up the bottle—or maybe they went to treatment and now they're right back at it again. It's maddening, heartbreaking, and absolutely exhausting to watch.

This happened before Steve ever agreed to go to treatment, during a time when we were still trying to make sense of what his drinking had done to his body. My husband was in the ICU in a coma for three months. I was so sure this would be a life-changing event. I convinced myself that when he woke up, he would count his blessings, realize how close he came to losing everything, and make the decision to change his ways. That belief kept me going during those long months.

One of the most frustrating aspects of loving someone with an addiction is that gap between what you hope will happen and what actually does. You think that after a DUI, a hospital stay, or a stint in treatment, things will finally change—but that's not always the case.

I remember sitting in support group meetings while Steve was in the ICU, gloating that I had his treatment facility picked out. I was basically rehearsing his recovery speech for him. In my mind, he'd be standing at a podium in ninety days, thanking me profusely for seeing him through. The Betty Ford facility had handsome pictures on their website, and I had already picked out his room.

The counselors running the meeting asked me multiple times if I was prepared for a letdown, and I just remember being confused as to why they would even say that to me. I was so wrapped up in my fantasy that I couldn't fathom that possibility.

Since we know recovery isn't linear and doesn't always go the way we think it will, it's going to be helpful for you to know how to manage those expectations. In this section, we will talk about how to use the tools to do just that so you're not constantly feeling disappointed and can start to see what really matters.

We know we can only control ourselves, our decisions, and our thoughts. You are now asking your loved one to self-reflect in order to change their behavior and move toward recovery, but it's now time for you to do your own self-reflection. It's time to remain in reality and not stay stuck on hope or some delusion of what you thought this recovery would look like. As you adjust your expectations, you're able to see things as they are and not what you thought they should be, and you're then able to see the progress as it's happening in real time.

Let's dive into how you can start doing this now.

Take a moment to ask yourself:

- What are my expectations when it comes to my loved one's recovery?

- Are these expectations reasonable based on where he's at now in his recovery?

- Are these expectations based on my hopes and wishes, or are they based on what he's shown to be possible and realistic?

Write these down and allow yourself some time to think about them. It's so important to be honest with yourself and to give yourself grace. If you realize your expectations are way off, that's okay. Recognizing that now is important.

Now, let's practice this with a brief exercise:

Think about one expectation you've had, such as: "I expect him not to drink once he says he's going to cut back."

Once you've set this expectation, ask yourself:

- Is this actually realistic?

- Is it something he's capable of?

- How did I come to the conclusion that this is realistic? What is it based on?

- What has he demonstrated to show that this is a realistic expectation?

- Why is this not a realistic expectation?

Now, write out your responses to these questions so you can then understand where you need to adjust. It's important to not just have expectations but also to reflect and understand where they came from.

How to Tell If Your Expectations Are Realistic

So, how do you know if your expectations are off? Well, think about your loved one's history. What have they shown they're capable of? Is there something in the way, such as another mental health issue? Sometimes, if there's a dual diagnosis, such as depression, this can further complicate the recovery process, especially if it's something that hasn't been addressed or treated.

If your expectations are based on what your loved one has shown in the past to be fully capable of, but there's a new development, like depression or anxiety that hasn't been diagnosed, then this could be something to consider. Recognizing this and adjusting your expectations can make the difference, and this can also be another explanation as to why there is a gap between what you think is possible and what actually is at the moment.

I don't want you to think that adjusting your expectations means lowering your standards or just accepting your loved one's behavior as acceptable. It's not about resigning to the fact that this is how things are. Adjusting your expectations simply means that the reality of the situation and where your loved one is in their journey doesn't match with your timeline. Sometimes, we're just off in our timing—and that's okay. Recovery is a process, and that process looks different for everyone. This disease is on a broad spectrum, and it's important to remain flexible and adaptable with the process.

You need to know that there will be setbacks. How many depends on the individual, but there can be multiple setbacks along the journey. It's normal.

Have you found yourself stuck, set on your expectations? This could show up in different ways. Maybe you're stuck on expectations like, "I expect him not to drink during outpatient treatment," or "I expect him to complete the full amount of time recommended by the admissions counselor." These are understandable hopes—but they're big expectations to have right out of the gate.

So, how do you know how far to bend without breaking? Let's talk about how to evaluate and adjust your expectations in a way that's realistic, healthy, and still hopeful.

Here's a checklist for you:

- Talk to a counselor who understands the current situation, not just your side of things.

- If there's a counselor working with the two of you, or if your loved one is involved in a treatment program, consider consulting with them just to check in.

- Evaluate the progress made so far and assess where your loved one might be limited right now.

- If you're new to this journey and haven't seen progress yet, keep an eye out for small improvements as you implement all the tools you're learning. If you're already in the midst of the journey, don't forget to acknowledge even the smallest strides your loved one has made and avoid comparing them to others. It's easy to look at someone else's progress and think, "But Susie's husband was able to quit drinking on his own with AA" or "Your friend went to treatment, and he's doing great now." There are so many factors at play, and this is a broad-spectrum disease. You can't compare one person to another and then decide where your loved one should be in their recovery.

It's a great idea to meet with a counselor who specializes in addiction to discuss where you are in your journey, evaluate the progress, and have a conversation about flexibility. Being flexible with your expectations will give both you and your loved one the grace you need as you move forward. It will relieve unnecessary pressure and make the process feel more manageable.

Quick Checklist

✓ Evaluate Progress Made So Far
  Think about and journal any—and I mean any—progress, big or small, that your loved one has made so you can reflect on it and see how far you've come.

✓ Talk to a Counselor Who Specializes in Addiction
  If there's a counselor working with your loved one, whether or not they're in a treatment program, talk to that person to check in and get feedback on the current state of the journey.

✓ Celebrate Small Wins
Look at the glass as half full, not half empty. When there's a win, celebrate it verbally and create rewards as you see fit.

✓ Avoid Comparing Yourself to Others
Don't compare yourself or your loved one to others going through the same journey. It's easy to think, "Well, Susie's husband quit drinking on his own with AA." But everyone's journey is different.

✓ Give Yourself and Your Loved One Grace
Neither one of you has all the answers, and that's okay. You're both going through this together.

A New Focus: Caring for Yourself

One of the most important things we haven't really touched on yet is self-care. You've probably heard the saying "Put on your air mask before you help others" many times, for good reason. If you're running on empty, you won't have the strength to support your loved one through this journey. That's why self-care isn't selfish—it's necessary. Even ten minutes a day can refill your emotional tank and keep you going.

You might feel like everything is going great, but then something unexpected happens. You need a clear mind, rest, and room for empathy and patience to respond, not react.

You might be thinking, "I don't have time for self-care." But making time is essential if you want to stay steady when the next challenge hits.

There are several ways to care for yourself, even if it's just for a few minutes each day. Since this needs to become part of your routine, pause and think about what you can do for yourself daily. Write down some self-care ideas that feel do-able for you. Here are some suggestions to get you started:

- Take a bath and bring a book.
- Call a friend and vent.
- Go on a walk.
- Journal
- Meditate or do some yoga.

It doesn't have to be complicated. I like to set a timer on my phone to remind me to take a few minutes for myself. It could be as simple as having a snack, watching TV, or stepping outside.

Eventually, I realized I needed to do it, or I wouldn't be able to keep going. There was a time when I didn't take care of myself and ended up in bed for days, unable to care for myself or my family. It takes less time to maintain your health than to try to regain it.

You deserve this. You need this.

This disease doesn't follow a straight path. Just like any chronic disease, addiction can have flare-ups, regressions, and breakthroughs. Preparing for that reality gives you power. This doesn't mean embracing a relapse with open arms and saying, "Oh well." It means preparing so you have a plan in place for when and if it does.

In the CRAFT method, there's something called the Two Steps Forward, One Step Back approach, so let's get right into that, along with an exercise to give you the tools to better prepare.

I find the Two Steps Forward, One Step Back approach to be an invaluable tool. The purpose of this method is to help the family member cope with setbacks when they happen, since we know recovery can be a roller coaster. Your loved one can have a long stretch of going along with the plan and then take a step back. This step back isn't something to be shocked by, and can look different for everyone.

A setback might be hard to recognize because it might start gradually. Maybe he missed one of his meetings, and now that missed meeting at the support group turns into several missed meetings. This is a setback because it's heading away from support and potentially toward other things that aren't as positive. It might mean he's hanging out at the bar again, which is also not in line with recovery.

And sometimes a setback is outright obvious—like returning to drinking, breaking a commitment, or a substance use binge.

Don't look at this as a failure on their part if this happens. This is simply an eye-opening experience, a time to learn from what happened so you can help guide him to do better the next time. It's a time to evaluate where things went wrong. This can mean you're able to evaluate this yourself, implement some safeguards, or meet with a counselor to help guide you through this.

CRAFT emphasizes not punishing your loved one when there is a setback, as this is not productive. CRAFT also recommends not overreacting. This means no pointing the finger, yelling, or making threats over this setback. It's so imperative to remain calm and collected, reflect on how far your loved one has come, and also remind them of that. Hold up that self-reflection mirror for your loved one to show them they've done this before and can do it again. Get back up and keep moving forward. If there's something in the plan that wasn't working, it can be adjusted.

Statements to reassure that you're on the same team and it's okay to get back up and try again are important. Try saying something like, "You've done amazing so far. I'm so impressed with all the work you've done, and I know we can get back on track." Your loved one really needs your reassurance at a time when they don't feel sure they're capable of getting through this

CRAFT also suggests that this step back—or possibly multiple steps back—might simply mean that a more intense treatment is in order, and it's time to discuss that if you haven't already. Sometimes, multiple stints at a treatment facility are needed, and that's okay.

Let's take a couple of minutes to do a quick exercise and reflect on a recent setback your loved one has had. I'll go first and remind you of the time my husband came back from detox, only to drink at the restaurant that night because he was "celebrating" his return from detox.

Now, ask yourself these questions:

- What did I learn from this?
- What overall positive changes have I seen in him despite this setback?
- What do I think prompted this setback?

Setting Small Goals That Actually Work

I suggest not just thinking about this but also writing it down so you can reflect on it later and revisit this. You can also take this exercise to a counselor and go over it with them.

Now, since we're looking at this with a glass-half-full perspective, write down some positive steps you've observed—whether that's their behavior, overall attitude, or any small actions that align with recovery.

Next, list any setbacks, even if they seem minor.

What you're doing here is reflecting on the Two Steps Forward, One Step Back approach. Looking back on this will help you visually see what has occurred and where you're at in this journey.

Now that you understand how to identify whether your expectations are realistic and how to manage expectations and setbacks, let's talk about setting goals that are manageable for you. Just like your loved one is tackling their addiction in small steps, you're going to break down your goals into small steps, too.

For example, instead of expecting that once your loved one acknowledges their problem, they'll suddenly stop drinking, a more realistic goal might be that they agree to talk to someone about it or attend a group meeting. Small changes lead to bigger ones, and it's important to keep that in mind.

To help you set these small, achievable goals, ask yourself the following:

- What is one thing I can set as a goal this month to change?
- What will I do to acknowledge those small changes when I see them?
- Is this goal realistic? Is it something that is doable based on where my loved one is right now in their journey?

It's important to keep your goals realistic and attainable so your loved one stays motivated. Doesn't it feel good when you reach a goal? It gives you the confidence to keep going and set the next one. Just like recovery, it's about taking things one step at a time.

Now that we've learned how to manage expectations and prepare for the setbacks that may come, it's time to move on to the next step: action. You now know everything that's needed to move forward, and if treatment is required, then an action plan is crucial. Together, we'll create a plan of action—exploring options, looking at the logistics, and bringing in family support. We'll talk about how to prepare, research, and discuss the challenges ahead.

The good news is that you're not alone. When Steve was struggling, I didn't have the family support I needed. People had their opinions that they shared through text or over the phone, but when I hung up, I was alone. Finding the right facility, doing the research to figure out what makes a treatment facility good, coming up with my plan, and implementing it— that was all on me. I didn't have a helping hand, but I want you to have one here with me. In the following chapter, I'll show you how to get through this part of the process. If you have friends and family you're close to, it's important to involve them in the journey.

We'll also look at statistics, and with the right plan and resources, you'll have everything.

Quick Recap: What You Can Start Using Today

✓ Take time to reflect on your expectations. Are they realistic, grounded in your loved one's current reality, or shaped by hope alone?

✓ Adjust your expectations to align with your loved one's actual progress, not the timeline you wish they were on.

✓ Keep the Two Steps Forward, One Step Back mindset to recognize growth without feeling defeated by setbacks.

✓ Journal to process emotions, gain perspective, and stay focused on your own growth.

✓ Make self-care a priority and part of your daily routine. Just a few minutes a day can make a big difference.

✓ Start small: set realistic goals for yourself and your loved one that feel doable, not overwhelming.

✓ Have a plan for how you'll handle setbacks so you can stay calm, prepared, and confident.

CHAPTER 14

How Do You Protect Your Children from the Effects of Addiction While Still Being There for the Addict?

This chapter was one of the hardest for me to write. It's about the ones who often get overlooked in the chaos: the children.

How Do You Protect Your Children from the Effects of Addiction While Still Being There for the Addict?

It was something I often asked myself, especially after realizing how deeply my children were affected by their father's addiction. I've shared with you the moments when my son stepped in to shield me and his sisters, acting far beyond his years in ways no child should ever have to. I've also shared how the addiction and the chaos it brought into our home escalated to the point where I had to obtain a restraining order.

Let me be clear: I'm not suggesting that obtaining a restraining order is the right choice for everyone, nor am I saying you have to choose between protecting your children and being there for the person you love who is struggling. What I want to do is share the tools I've learned so that you can protect everyone involved—including your children—because I truly believe it's possible to find a balance that supports both.

At the time, I was in survival mode—trying to save my husband's life, maintain a sense of normalcy for my children, and juggle work along with the everyday responsibilities of life. I was stretched so thin that I couldn't fully see the impact Steve's addiction was having on my kids until much later. Looking back now, I realize there are things I could have done differently. That's why I want to share what I've learned with you so you can take steps to help your children now.

Addiction doesn't just affect the person struggling with it; it seeps into the lives of everyone in the household, especially children. Whether or not your children are vocalizing their thoughts and feelings, they are absorbing everything like sponges. They feel the stress, unpredictability, and pain that addiction brings. The question isn't whether they're affected—it's about how we address it, minimize the harm, and empower them to feel safe and supported.

1. Give Yourself Grace
   Recognizing how addiction impacts your children—or other loved ones in the household—can bring a wave of guilt. You may find yourself asking, "How did I let this happen?" or "Why didn't I notice sooner?" These feelings are normal. But it's important not to get stuck in them.

   No one expects you to be perfect. You're navigating an incredibly difficult situation—trying to care for someone with an addiction while also protecting your children and managing your own responsibilities. It's an overwhelming balancing act, and it's okay to admit that.

Instead of focusing on what you feel you could have done differently, focus on the progress you're making now. Remind yourself daily that you're doing the best you can with the information and tools you have at this moment. Every step you take to support your loved one also supports your children and the family as a whole. Progress, no matter how small, is still progress.

2. Help Your Children Understand That Addiction Doesn't Define Their Loved One

Children often internalize the behavior of the person struggling with addiction, especially when that behavior is hurtful or inappropriate. If the addict's anger, frustration, or unpredictable actions are directed at the children, they may start to believe they've done something wrong or that they're to blame. Over time, this can erode their self-esteem, create anxiety, and even lead to depression or post-traumatic stress.

It's critical to help your children understand that the person they love and the behaviors caused by addiction are not the same. Be honest with them in a way that's appropriate for their age and emotional maturity.

For young children (ages one–ten):

Even toddlers and preschoolers can sense when something isn't right, even if they can't fully verbalize it. My youngest daughter, for instance, started acting out and throwing tantrums as a toddler in connection with the ups and downs of the addiction. She didn't have the words to express her confusion and fear, but she desperately needed comfort and reassurance.

Use simple and clear language. You might say:

"Your dad loves you so much, and that will never change. But when he drinks, it makes him act differently and say things he doesn't mean. It's never your fault, and you are so loved."

For older children or teens (ages eleven and above):

Older kids can understand more about the disease of addiction. Sharing age-appropriate educational materials or explaining what you know about alcoholism can help them make sense of what they're seeing. The goal is to give them context that fosters empathy and understanding without excusing harmful behaviors.

You might say:

"I know you've noticed how your dad acts when he's been drinking. Alcohol can make people behave in ways that aren't true to who they are. If your dad yells or takes his anger out on you, those words don't reflect his real feelings—it's the alcohol talking. That doesn't mean he doesn't love you or that you've done anything wrong. If you ever want to talk about how you're feeling, I'm here to listen."

Reassure them often. Children need repetition to process and believe what you're telling them. Revisiting these conversations regularly will help reinforce their sense of security and self-worth.

3. Create Structure and Routine

While you can't always control the chaos that addiction brings into a household, you can create structure for your children, and children thrive on structure. Even if they tell you they don't like it, kids take comfort in knowing what to expect. Predictability helps them feel secure.

Here are some ways to create structure:

- Establish daily routines. Create a schedule that includes everyday tasks like breakfast, getting ready for school, homework, dinner, bath time, and bedtime. Include scheduled bonding time, like reading a book, watching a favorite show, playing a game, or simply sitting and talking together.

- Maintain household rules. It's tempting to relax rules out of guilt, like skipping chores or letting things slide, but consistency is important. It creates a sense of normalcy and teaches kids that expectations don't disappear during difficult times.

- Plan special family moments. Go beyond daily bonding time and plan outings like a hike, a picnic, or a movie night. Having something to look forward to as a family provides a sense of connection and joy. If your loved one is still drinking or struggling with consistency, choose activities that feel manageable and low-pressure. You don't have to plan something elaborate—sometimes a simple meal at home, a short walk, or a board game can be just as meaningful. Try to pick times of day when your loved one is more likely to be sober or emotionally present so everyone can enjoy the experience together.

4. Validate Their Feelings

Each child processes the chaos of addiction differently, depending on their age and personality. Even if they don't verbalize their emotions, it's important to create a safe space where they feel comfortable expressing themselves.

Start with open-ended questions, such as:

- "How have you been feeling about everything at home?"
- "Is there anything going on that's been bothering you?"

- Reassure them that their feelings are normal. You might say:
- "It's okay to feel upset or angry. Those feelings are normal, and I feel them, too, sometimes. It's important to talk about them, and I'm always here to listen."

If they're hesitant to open up, acknowledge their difficulty. You could say:

"I know it's hard to share your feelings. I struggle with that sometimes, too. But I want you to know that you can tell me anything, and I'll never judge you. I love you no matter what."

5. Recognize Behavioral Changes and Seek Support

Sometimes, children may not verbalize their struggles, but their behavior can reveal their feelings. Look for changes such as frequent tantrums, withdrawing from family or friends, or trouble at school. If you notice significant shifts in their behavior, it's important to address them.

Here are some steps you can take:

- Speak with a school counselor or teacher who interacts with your child daily.
- Connect with a therapist who can provide a safe space for them to process their emotions.
- Talk to your pediatrician for additional resources or recommendations.

It's normal to feel apprehensive about involving outside support when you're trying to protect your loved one with an addiction. But addressing your child's needs is crucial. With the right professionals, you can ensure your family receives the support it needs without judgment.

You can protect your children while navigating the challenges of addiction. By giving yourself grace, helping your children separate the person from the disease, creating structure, validating their feelings, and recognizing when to seek help. Together, you can create an environment of love, security, and hope.

Reflection Journal: Supporting Your Children Through Addiction

Take a few moments to reflect and write:

- What is one thing you've noticed about how your child or children are emotionally affected by your loved one's addiction?
  (Think about behavioral changes, emotional outbursts, withdrawing, school issues, or signs of anxiety.)

- Have you talked to your children about addiction in an age-appropriate way? If not, what's holding you back?
  (Write out what's been stopping you and what you wish you could say if you felt ready.)

- What is one simple thing you can do this week to create more structure or security for your children?
  (Think small: a consistent bedtime routine, dedicated one-on-one time, a calm family check-in, or even just being present.)

- What support might you or your child need right now, and how can you begin to provide that?
  (This could be counseling, journaling, a conversation with a trusted adult, or simply carving out more quality time.)

CHAPTER 15

Creating Your
Treatment Action Plan

You've come this far, learning all the necessary tools. That's the groundwork. It's time to create a plan and take the next step toward helping your loved one. This chapter is all about taking that crucial step into action.

Let's dive into your action plan so you'll know how to research treatment options, handle the logistics of getting your loved one into treatment, and prepare for what comes next.

Now that you're exploring treatment options, knowing what to look for is incredibly important. I know you want the best for your loved one, so once they agree to enter treatment, it's crucial to make sure it's a good fit. The facility needs to offer care that meets your loved one's unique needs. Addiction isn't one-size-fits-all, and neither is recovery. That's true for both inpatient and outpatient programs.

When the facility is the right fit, the likelihood of success is much greater. So, let's talk about how to gather the information you need to make that decision.

Here are a few key things to consider as you research treatment facilities:

1. Accreditation

   Accreditation means the facility meets the standards set by a trusted governing body. Look for accreditation from the Joint Commission (JCO), the Commission on Accreditation of Rehabilitation Facilities (CARF), or the National Association of Addiction Treatment Providers (NAATP). That's a great place to start.

   You can also use tools like Psychology Today and SAMHSA's treatment locator to help narrow your search. What I like about SAMHSA is that you can filter by location, level of care, and specific treatment types—like detox, inpatient, or outpatient programs. Psychology Today is also user-friendly and easy to navigate.

2. Treatment Modalities

   Each facility uses different approaches to treatment. Ask what modalities they offer and do a little research to make sure they align with your loved one's needs.

   If AA or traditional therapy hasn't worked in the past, look for programs that include other options, like individual, group, or family therapy, or holistic therapies, such as mindfulness, yoga, or art. If you're not sure what would be best, speak with a professional who specializes in addiction.

   Many treatment centers use a combination of methods. Some of the most effective include:

   - Motivational Interviewing
   - Cognitive Behavioral Therapy (CBT)
   - Dialectical Behavioral Therapy (DBT)
   - Holistic approaches that support mind-body healing

The CRAFT method is also becoming more common. It's an especially powerful tool because it bridges the gap between what the patient is experiencing and how family members are coping. When a facility uses CRAFT and includes you in your loved one's care plan, it gives you a chance to sharpen your tools and start building the next phase of recovery—together.

3. Staff Qualifications
Ask about the qualifications of the staff. Licensed substance abuse counselors should have credentials like LADC or CADC, which show certification through recognized organizations. Don't hesitate to ask about their training, therapeutic approach, and even the staff-to-patient ratio. These things matter.

4. Success Rates
No facility can promise recovery. Even the best treatment center can't control timing or readiness. It sometimes takes more than one try, and that's okay.
You may see "success rates" listed on websites, but those often reflect program completion, not long-term sobriety. Still, they can offer helpful insight. Many people leave early for reasons that have nothing to do with the quality of care, like being too close to home, not feeling ready, or lacking family support.
That's why it's just as important to look at reviews and testimonials. Ask:
- Did other families feel supported?
- Were they given tools that helped during and after treatment?

- Did the environment feel safe, respectful, and hopeful?

Once you've found the right facility, the next step is to implement your plan. This will take some organization, but don't worry—you're not doing this alone. I'm here to help you, and with a bit of preparation, you can do this.

> Timing is everything. Once your loved one agrees to enter treatment, it's important to act fast—before doubt, fear, or denial has a chance to creep in. Have everything lined up beforehand so there's no delay. Ideally, by the time they say yes, you've already chosen the facility, gotten insurance approval, asked your questions, and planned everything out accordingly.

In most cases, the next step after that would be an assessment, and that's when the critical window begins. There's often a short window of opportunity between the assessment and actual admission, and this is where many people back out.

Some facilities have long waitlists, while others can admit new patients within a few days. In many cases, by the time your loved one reaches the point of saying "yes" to help and completes the intake assessment, you've already moved past much of the waiting period. From my experience, private treatment centers usually have shorter wait times than state-funded programs.

Government-funded centers may be more affordable, but they often come with trade-offs, like longer delays, fewer resources, less individualized care, and stricter program requirements. It's important to weigh these factors when you're researching treatment options, so you can be prepared and realistic about what to expect. Ask yourself, "How urgently is treatment needed?"

Studies have shown that when treatment doesn't happen quickly, a large percentage of people back out, sometimes before even making it to their first appointment.[21] That's why preparation matters so much. The sooner you can get your loved one into treatment after they say yes, the better your chances of follow-through and long-term success.

Think Ahead About Transportation

This is a scary time. Your loved one is walking into treatment not knowing when they'll return home. And that's true whether the facility is local or out of state. Your loved one needs support, reassurance, and someone to hold them accountable in those critical few moments as they leave the house, get in the car, and make their way there. They're often looking for an out the whole way.

How will your loved one get there? If the facility is local, great. But if it's out of state, who will accompany them? Is it you? Or is it another family member or trusted friend?

If you can't go, ideally, someone close to them—someone calm and encouraging—can make the trip. Even just being there during intake can help ease the transition. Many facilities also offer transportation services or can help arrange third-party support. Just be sure to ask about this ahead of time.

Also, think through practical details like flights, layovers, what to pack, and how to handle emotional goodbyes. This is where your plan begins to feel real—for both of you. Your calm presence, even in small ways, can help your loved one walk through that door with confidence.

Planning Ahead: What About Childcare, Pets, and Tasks at Home?

When your loved one enters treatment—especially inpatient care—it's easy to focus on finding the right facility, transportation, and insurance. But what about the everyday tasks that keep your household running smoothly?

If your loved one typically helps with daily routines, you'll need to think through how those responsibilities will be handled while they're away. Things like childcare, feeding pets, coordinating kids' activities, or managing bills and mail may need to shift temporarily.

Ask yourself:

- Who will help take care of the kids, pets, or household tasks?
- Are there appointments, payments, or school responsibilities I need to take over?
- Is there anyone I need to notify?
- Do I have access to important info—like passwords or online banking—to manage things smoothly?

Creating a shared calendar or checklist before treatment begins can help ensure nothing is missed. Taking care of these loose ends ahead of time reduces stress for you, lowers anxiety for your loved one, and removes one more excuse not to follow through.

Before Steve entered treatment, I made a list of everything I was worried about. My son had basketball and football practice during the week. My daughters went to different schools. I was working full-time, and my job was thirty minutes from home. Managing all of that alone felt overwhelming at first, but making a list of what would need to be done and receiving help from others took the pressure off.

Once I created the calendar, I reached out to my support system and asked where they could step in. Neighbors offered rides. Friends delivered meals. I took over the bills. It worked out—but only because I took the time to plan ahead. You can, too.

Financial Planning and Paying for Treatment

Once you've worked out the timing and logistics, it's important to consider the financial side of treatment. Most health insurance policies cover some portion of inpatient or outpatient care, but the details vary by policy. I purchased a private plan because the recommended facility was listed as in-network. But when I called my insurance company, I found out it wasn't covered, so I reached out to an insurance broker who helped me find a plan that fit our needs. I recommend doing the same.

Start by calling your insurance provider and asking which facilities are in-network—both in-state and out-of-state—and what your out-of-pocket costs will be. Then talk to the facility about the remaining balance. Ask if they offer financial aid, payment plans, or sliding-scale fees based on income. You can also ask friends or family to contribute or use a platform like GoFundMe.

There are almost always options. Don't let cost be the thing that stands in the way of recovery.

Once the logistics and finances are in place, the next challenge is finding the right facility—one that truly fits your loved one's needs. Here's what that process looked like for us.

My Personal Experience with Finding the Right Facility

When I found Betty Ford, I knew it was the right place. They specialized in dual diagnosis, which was crucial for Steve's needs, and they tailored the treatment plan to meet all his unique challenges. The staff was kind and professional. They had doctors and nurses on-site during detox, which gave me peace of mind knowing he'd be safe.

In my opinion, Steve not completing the program at Betty Ford wasn't a reflection on the facility at all. Betty Ford is an excellent center. The truth was that Steve just wasn't ready yet in his journey—and I've come to accept that.

Recovery isn't a straight road forward, and sometimes even the best treatment facility doesn't yield immediate results. But it does give you the best chance for success and provides valuable tools that your loved one needs. The important thing is to find the facility that provides the necessary support and that, when your loved one leaves, he's armed with new tools to make it at home with confidence and the hope to move forward.

Another major concern—especially for the person entering treatment—is how to manage work and job security during this time.

Taking Leave from Work

This is one of the biggest challenges, not necessarily because an employer won't allow time off but because of the fear surrounding it. Many people worry that if they admit they need time off for substance abuse treatment, they'll lose their job. That fear alone can stop someone from moving forward with a treatment plan, either because they feel paralyzed by it or use it as the next excuse not to get help.

There are a few ways to handle this. You don't have to disclose that it's a substance issue. Saying there's a mental health crisis is often enough. They're not going to pry or ask for details. Most HR departments are required to keep this information confidential. In fact, some employers may even help cover the cost of treatment, so it's worth looking into.

Once your loved one has had their intake appointment, you'll have a better idea of how much time off is needed. This can vary depending on the severity of the addiction. If your loved one has been at their job for a year or more, they may qualify for FMLA—the Family and Medical Leave Act—which protects their job for up to three months. Additional leave may be available, too, so it's worth speaking directly with HR.

I've thought about this so many times. It still haunts me because I truly believe that if I had recognized how much leaving work was a barrier for Steve, he might still be here today.

Looking back, I now believe he chose detox because it felt manageable. A quick fix. He had a moment of clarity, thought, "Okay, I have a problem," and believed he could just detox, get sober, and handle the rest on his own.

But Steve also carried the weight of supporting our family. And because of that, he couldn't see past the short term. He couldn't imagine taking three or six months off to get better. He never considered the bigger picture: that if he didn't get better—really better—he might not be here at all, and that without treatment, he wouldn't be able to support us ever again.

I didn't know then what I know now. I couldn't see the full picture. I was unprepared—and painfully unaware.

But now I do. And that's why I'm telling you. This piece right here is critical. The fear of losing a job or stepping away from work is real, but so is the risk of losing everything if treatment doesn't happen.

If your loved one is feeling anxious, don't ignore it—talk about it. Remind them of my story. Let them know you've already come up with solutions to help ease their fears and that they don't have to worry about everything falling apart.

Reassure them: you've thought this through, and they won't be going through it alone.

Finding or Building a Support Network

You cannot do this alone, and you shouldn't have to. Having people you can turn to is not just helpful; it's necessary. Support is what keeps you going when continuing feels impossible, especially when your loved one's situation becomes overwhelming.

When things were at their worst with Steve, I leaned on a couple of close friends, but most of the time, I felt completely alone. I didn't want to burden people with my personal issues, and I was afraid I'd push them away. But this is what friends and family are for—to be there in your darkest hour and to show up when you need them.

I desperately wanted my in-laws to be involved, to help Steve stay accountable and be part of the recovery plan, but I never got that. Steve had them convinced I was exaggerating. Despite his ICU visits and the empty vodka bottles, they refused to see the truth. Looking back, I understand why: it's easier to stay in denial when the problem is your own child. And they were still actively drinking, too.

His brothers didn't show up either. One was battling addiction himself, and the other, I believe, distanced himself to protect his own emotional stability. I felt like I was in a sink-hole with no one to help pull me out. I wish I had reached out to a counselor sooner—someone who could've helped me navigate those difficult relationships and given me the strength to keep going.

If this sounds like your family, know that you're not alone. It's more common than you think. And it's even more reason to build your own support system—whether it's with friends, neighbors, online groups, or a trusted therapist.

I found Facebook groups to be a lifesaver. I didn't have to leave home or rearrange my life. I could log in anytime and find connection and encouragement. These groups became a safe space to vent, process feelings, or simply have someone listen, especially on nights when I didn't want to call anyone but still needed to feel heard.

If you do have supportive family members, lean on them. Let them in. And if they're open to it, invite them to join a support group with you. Having a team beside you helps you stay strong, clear, and focused when it matters most, especially when your loved one comes home from treatment, and the real work begins.

Having support isn't just critical when trying to get your loved one to treatment—it's just as critical when they return home. Treatment is only one part of the journey. The real work starts once they're back in the environment where the addiction took hold.

Even after treatment, there are still temptations, stressors, and emotional triggers at home. Your loved one may have learned helpful tools and started to heal, but the brain doesn't recover overnight. This disease hasn't gone into full remission; it still requires management and support every day.

That's why preparing for what comes next is so important. Here's a simple aftercare checklist to help you plan for their return and keep moving forward together.

Aftercare Checklist: What Comes Next

1. Daily Check-In

   This doesn't have to be formal. In fact, I wouldn't make it formal because then your loved one will feel like you're babysitting them and that they have no freedom, which can create more stress. Instead, just casually ask them how they're feeling and if they need anything, and just make yourself available. Ask loved ones and friends to do this, too.

2. Support Groups

   Find a support group that the two of you can attend. This might be together or separately, depending on the group. Encourage other family members to attend as well.

3. Additional Therapy

   Have pre-scheduled therapy sessions for both of you—together and separately—so that both of you can continue to get the support you need.

4. Accountability System

   It's important that your loved one has someone they can call when they feel the temptation to dabble back into their old habits. Someone who can talk them through this. This can be someone else in recovery, a family member, or a counselor.

5. New Healthy Routine

   Old habits can eventually be replaced when new

habits are formed, such as exercise, meditation, yoga, or a healthy diet. Find something that supports emotional and mental health.

6. Emergency Plan
Since we know there's a chance of relapse, it's important to have an emergency plan in place. This could include a return to the treatment facility, having another treatment facility on standby, entering outpatient treatment, or a same-day emergency meeting with a healthcare professional.

7. Communication
Talk openly together with your loved one about challenges that might come up. Don't just listen—actively listen to really hear those potential challenges and concerns. Do so without placing blame or judgment.

The Urgency of Early Action

The longer you wait to get your loved one the help they need, the harder it becomes for recovery to take place. I truly believe this is the reason Steve isn't here today. He didn't make it, and though I carry no anger toward him or myself, I would have done things differently knowing what I know now.

That's why I urge you—don't wait any longer. You don't need to wait for everything to get worse or for the red flags to become impossible to ignore. Act now while you still have the opportunity to intervene.

Studies and real-world outcomes continue to show that early intervention leads to better results. When action is taken early—before the addiction becomes more deeply rooted—there's a much stronger chance for long-term recovery.

The longer you wait, the harder it becomes. The behavior is more deeply ingrained, the physical toll is greater, and the emotional and psychological damage spreads wider.

Early intervention can also prevent the addiction from spiraling into serious, sometimes irreversible consequences. It reduces the risk of legal trouble, like a DUI or an arrest, and helps your loved one avoid life-altering events like a car accident while under the influence. It lowers the chance of permanent health complications—things like liver disease, diabetes, stroke, neurological damage, cancer, and death.

Waiting also allows addiction to become more complex, often layered with trauma, emotional instability, and physical decline. And while recovery is always possible, the longer it's delayed, the harder it is to untangle the web of damage and get back to a healthy baseline.

You have everything you need to create a plan. The most important thing I want to stress—the reason I wrote this book for you—is the importance of quick intervention.

Don't be afraid of sounding silly, overreacting, or being too quick to sound the alarm. There's really no such thing. Others—including your loved one—might make you feel like you're overreacting, but you know better. You don't need to justify your feelings to anyone.

What you do need is support. Take action now so you can find peace—and so everyone involved can begin to heal. The tools are all here, laid out before you. You can do this—and anything you set your mind to.

Reflection Journal: Creating and Acting on Your Treatment Plan
Now, take a moment to reflect and write:

- What is one thing that's been holding you back from helping your loved one take that leap toward treatment? *(Is it fear of their reaction, financial concerns, or not knowing where to start?)*

- Assuming your loved one is ready, what's one step you can take this week to start preparing for treatment? *(This could be researching facilities, calling your insurance company, or jotting down questions to ask.)*

- What is it that you need right now to help you move forward? *(Think about who you can count on for support—friends, family, online groups, a counselor, or even just scheduling time for yourself.)*

- What's something you can delegate to get off your plate? *(Transportation, meals, help with the kids, help with house chores. Write out what help you need and who might be able to step in.)*

- What will you do to remind yourself why you're doing this, even when it gets hard? *(This could be journaling, posting a quote, or setting a daily intention.)*

CHAPTER 16

The Long Game: Supporting Recovery One Day at a Time

Look how far you've come. You've dedicated your time and energy to understanding this disease and showing the courage to take action. This journey isn't easy, but willingness, knowledge, and consistency are already half the battle.

I've shared everything I know so you can take it and make a difference. If I'd had these tools earlier, I truly believe Steve's story might have ended differently. We didn't find them until the eleventh hour, when the damage to his body was too great. The tools worked. I saw real changes in him. But we had simply run out of time. That's not where you are. You're still on this journey, and now is the time to act. Both of you can take steps to get your life back.

We've talked about the potential for setbacks, and while relapse can happen, it doesn't mean all is lost. Recovery doesn't stop the moment your loved one comes home or says they're ready to change—it's a process. But with the right resources, tools, and safeguards in place, long-term healing is absolutely possible.

I'm not saying the burden is on you, but you are the steady support—the constant—the one that holds a lot of power and influence. The goal here is progress, not perfection. It's not your job to fix this.

What Long-Term Recovery Looks Like

To foster long-term recovery, I want you to picture what that looks like. What comes to mind? Maybe you think of forever sobriety, peace in your home, or finally feeling hopeful again. That's possible, but it requires an environment that truly supports it. Consider the following building blocks:

Routine
Create a daily schedule that supports wellness. This can include healthy sleep and eating habits, mindfulness exercises or meditation, and taking prescribed medications as directed.

Emotional Health

Make sure your loved one has access to mental health support—whether that means a therapist, support group, or regular check-ins with a doctor. Addressing anxiety, depression, or other challenges is essential to their recovery.

Healthy Activities

Encourage activities that bring joy, purpose, and movement, like joining a gym, taking up a hobby, going on walks, or spending time with friends. These distractions are productive and healing.

How You Can Help Sustain Sobriety

Encourage your loved one to maintain their network of care—whether that means attending support groups, therapy, or both. Even if they say, "I'm doing fine" or "I don't need this anymore," consistency is key. Support is most important when things seem stable because that's often when setbacks quietly begin.

Maintain Accountability
Hold your loved one accountable for their recovery in a supportive way. This doesn't mean controlling them; it means encouraging them to follow through on their commitments. You can do this by gently checking in.

- Ask how their support meetings are going.
- Remind them of their own goals and progress.
- Celebrate their achievements—big or small.
- If they start to slip, calmly ask if something is bothering them or if they need support.

Accountability isn't about pressure; it's about being a consistent, loving presence who believes in their ability to change.

Celebrate Progress—Big and Small

Acknowledge your loved one's strength and determination. Remind them you're proud of their effort, no matter how small the win. These moments deserve recognition. Depending on the achievement, you can celebrate in a way that feels meaningful—whether it's a night out, a small getaway, or something simple like takeout and a movie at home. Make it about connection and encouragement, not pressure.

Maintain Healthy Boundaries

Your boundaries matter just as much now as they did before, maybe even more. As your loved one works toward recovery, it can be tempting to ease up, but that's when old patterns can sneak back in. Adjust your boundaries as needed, but make sure they remain clear, consistent, and firm. Boundaries protect both of you, creating a safe space for healing and growth.

Promote Self-Sufficiency

You've done so much, but now it's time for your loved one to take the reins. Recovery isn't just about getting sober; it's about building a life they can manage confidently. That means they should be the one scheduling their therapy appointments, attending meetings, and making decisions that support their sobriety. This doesn't mean you stop supporting them. It means you're stepping back enough for them to step forward.

Make the Home a Recovery-Friendly Space

The environment your loved one returns to plays a major role in their recovery. A calm, consistent, and supportive home can make all the difference.

Here are some simple ways to minimize triggers and create a recovery-friendly home:

- Remove alcohol from the home.

- Avoid drinking around your loved one. Ask family and friends to do the same.

- Throw away any leftover bottles or cans. Don't let visual reminders linger.

- Choose media carefully. Opt for TV shows and movies that don't glamorize drinking or substance use.

- Maintain a predictable routine. Structure helps reduce stress and gives a sense of stability.

Some of the most powerful triggers aren't physical objects—they're emotional stressors or unpredictable routines. That's why a calm, consistent home environment can make such a difference. Try creating a simple family routine that reduces stress and brings a sense of normalcy. Keep things supportive and peaceful whenever possible.

You're not alone in this journey. Just because your loved one is out of treatment doesn't mean your support ends—it's even more critical now. This is the time when ongoing support makes the biggest difference.

It's also normal to feel like you've already drained so much energy from those around you and that they're ready to move on, but this isn't true either. If you feel this way, you might be mirroring your own feelings of exhaustion onto others.

Let your family members and friends be there for you. Don't automatically decide that everyone is done and ready to move on. If this journey is still continuing in your life, let them be part of it. Share your feelings and delegate as you need to. We all get busy with work, kids, and other responsibilities, and it's okay to ask for help or take a break when you need one.

Building a strong circle of support is one of the most important steps you can take for both you and your loved one. Here's how you can do it and why it makes a difference.

Look for local recovery groups in your community. You can do this by googling local support groups in your area or joining an online support group where you can participate from the comfort of your home. Reach out to others in your area who are willing to lend a helping hand.

I leaned heavily on my community. I was attending church regularly during this time and shared with some members what I was going through. They showed up in an unbelievable way. I had meals delivered to my door when I was in the thick of it. Other mothers offered to babysit so that I could get some things done.

People can't help you if they don't know what's going on. There are so many wonderful people willing to lend a helping hand if you allow them.

Issues may come up in the future, so having an established counselor you can call or schedule an appointment with—someone who already knows the two of you and your situation—can be incredibly helpful. This counselor can continue to guide you through your success.

Who's your accountability team? This could be:

- A group of friends who check in with your loved one regularly.

- A sponsor.

- A doctor or therapist.

These people play an important role in helping your loved one stay on track while also providing you with support when needed.

Setbacks are part of any journey. They're not failures; they're moments of learning and adjusting. A setback might mean you were in a good place, communicating well, and now you're not. Or it might mean your loved one was staying consistent with meetings and taking care of their health, but lately, those habits are slipping.

This is normal, and it can happen once we get comfortable. Sometimes we stick with something for a while and then decide "Things are going so well that I don't need to do these actions anymore," like attending meetings, meditating, or keeping counseling appointments. That's often when setbacks occur. In fact, setbacks may happen even if you're doing everything "right."

But here's the good news: as you work through these setbacks, you'll become more resilient. You'll come out stronger than ever before—a changed person, capable of handling whatever comes your way. All the tools you've learned throughout this journey apply not just to addiction but also to life. They'll serve you in parenting, relationships, work, and everyday challenges.

When you understand that setbacks are part of the process, you stop seeing them as failures. Instead, you see them for what they are: opportunities for growth and redirection.

So, what do you do when a setback happens?

Revisit your plan. Reassess. Take a moment to pause, breathe, and have an honest conversation—with yourself and with your loved one. Ask what's working, what's not, and why. Then reach out to your support team, whether that's a counselor, a trusted friend, or a family member, to help you process, brainstorm, and regain your clarity so you can pivot forward.

Go back to your journal entries and read what you've written. Remind yourself where you started and how far you've come. Revisit the wins you captured in those pages—those moments of strength, courage, and progress. Let those reflections ground you in how much growth has already happened.

From there, the two of you can commit to a new plan. Maybe your current plan just needs a few tweaks. Or maybe it's time for a brand-new one. Either way, that's okay. You are not starting over; you're building on experience.

You have help all around you. Support groups, counselors, family members, and friends—they're all there to help catch you in the fall.

And I want to say this clearly: I am so proud of you. You made it through these steps, and regardless of where you are in the journey, you've come a long way. The fact that you picked up this book, read through every chapter, and did the work—that is a win. Because knowledge is power. And now you have it.

Recovery is possible. My story doesn't have a happy ending, but it carries a powerful lesson: early intervention and consistent support can change everything.

But I also shared Jane's story, a story of recovery and hope. Her commitment to the CRAFT method, her steady support, and her love brought her family through to the other side. That can be your story, too.

You now have the tools in your hands to create real, lasting change. And, most importantly, you are never alone.

I want you to take what you've learned and put it into practice. This is all about trying and trusting the process. It's never about being perfect. You, and only you, have the power to produce change, and it starts with you.

Remember to focus on small steps, lean on your community, and know that if you're coming from a place of love, that's what matters most. You're on your way to healing and building a new future.

Reflection Journal: Committing to Long-Term Recovery

- Have you pictured what long-term recovery looks like and how can you support that vision?
  (Think about structure, boundaries, treatment routines, and emotional support.)

- What are three things you've learned through this journey that you don't want to forget and want to share with others?
  (These could be tools or a change in mindset.)

- What support do you need in the long term as you progress, and who can you ask for help?
  (List people, groups, or professionals who can walk with you through this next chapter.)

- What will you do when you experience a setback, and how will you remind yourself that it's not the end of the world or an ultimate failure?
  (Write down your go-to plan.)

Acknowledgments

I want to thank Dr. Timothy J. Fernstrom for being a constant support. He was the attending medical doctor every time Steve went into the ICU. He not only treated him with compassionate care but never judged me for the medical decisions I made. He was a steady presence and a source of strength during the most difficult moments.

To Michelle Kuecker, for generously sharing your expertise, contributing your insights, and writing the foreword for this book. Your guidance and the work you do every day to help families make lasting changes inspired and informed so much of what's written here. (If you'd like to connect with Michelle, she can be reached at michelle.kuecker@gmail.com.)

To Dr. Robert J. Meyers and the late Dr. Nathan Azrin, for developing the CRAFT method and paving the way for real change in the way families approach addiction. Your work has impacted countless lives, including mine.

To Ashley Mansour for your guidance and encouragement throughout this writing process, and to your entire team—including the editors—for helping me bring this book to life.

To my family, for providing unwavering support during this intense season of writing and for giving me the space to accomplish this goal.

To the countless family members who are still walking this journey with someone they love—this book is for you.

And finally, I never thought I would acknowledge myself—but I also never thought I would climb out of the state of emotional turmoil I was in, let alone write a book. So I want to thank myself for doing the self-work, for pushing through to the other side, and for showing up so that you can also see that the other side is possible.

thehardesthelp.com

About the Author

Holly Thorton is a writer, entrepreneur, and mother of four, known for her compassionate and practical approach to helping families navigate the challenges of supporting a loved one struggling with alcoholism. After losing her husband to alcoholism, Holly realized that the resources she desperately needed were scattered and incomplete. She couldn't find one book that offered both the raw, honest experience of living with addiction and the practical tools to guide a loved one toward recovery.

So, she wrote the book she wished she'd had—a book that combines heartfelt storytelling with actionable advice. As the creator of The Hardest Help, Holly offers education, support, and guidance to those who feel lost in the chaos of a loved one's addiction. Her mission is to provide hope, understanding, and real-world solutions for those who feel alone.

Holly's experience taught her that even in the darkest moments, there is always a path forward. She is passionate about helping others find that path, arming them with knowledge, support, and the courage to take the next step.

There is no perfect way to help someone you love, but there is a better way. She hopes this book becomes that guide for you.

To contact the author regarding speaking engagements, media inquiries, or any questions you may have, please go to: www.thehardesthelp.com

Endnotes

1. National Institute on Alcohol Abuse and Alcoholism. *Alcohol Use Disorder: A Chronic Relapsing Brain Disease.* Bethesda, MD: National Institutes of Health, 2021. https://www.niaaa.nih.gov/alcohols-effects-health/alcohol-use-disorder

2. National Institute on Alcohol Abuse and Alcoholism. *Alcohol Withdrawal Syndrome.* Bethesda, MD: National Institutes of Health, 2021. https://www.niaaa.nih.gov

3. National Institute on Alcohol Abuse and Alcoholism. "Genetics of Alcohol Use Disorder." *NIAAA,* https://www.niaaa.nih.gov/publications/brochures-and-fact-sheets/genetics-alcohol-use-disorder

4. Substance Abuse and Mental Health Services Administration (SAMHSA) and National Institute on Alcohol Abuse and Alcoholism (NIAAA). *National Survey on Drug Use and Health.* Rockville, MD: SAMHSA, 2023. https://www.niaaa.nih.gov

5. National Institute on Drug Abuse. *Principles of Drug Addiction Treatment: A Research-Based Guide (Third Edition).* U.S. Department of Health and Human Services, 2018. https://nida.nih.gov/publications/principles-drug-addiction-treatment-research-based-guide-third-edition

6. National Institute on Drug Abuse. *Principles of Drug Addiction Treatment: A Research-Based Guide (Third*

*Edition).*National Institutes of Health, U.S. Department of Health and Human Services, 2018. https://nida.nih. gov/publications/principles-drug-addiction-treatment-research-based-guide-third-edition

7. National Institute on Alcohol Abuse and Alcoholism (NIAAA). "Alcohol Use Disorder: A Comparison Between DSM–IV and DSM–5." *niaaa.nih.gov.* Accessed August 6, 2025. https://www.niaaa.nih.gov/alcohols-effects-health/professionals-dsm-5-comparison

8. American Psychiatric Association. *Diagnostic and Statistical Manual of Mental Disorders, Fifth Edition (DSM-5).* Arlington, VA: American Psychiatric Publishing, 2013.

9. National Institute on Alcohol Abuse and Alcoholism (NIAAA). "Alcohol Use Disorder (AUD) Assessment." *niaaa.nih.gov.* Accessed 2023. https://www.niaaa.nih.gov

10. National Institute on Alcohol Abuse and Alcoholism (NIAAA). *Treatment for Alcohol Problems: Finding and Getting Help.* Bethesda, MD: National Institutes of Health, U.S. Department of Health and Human Services, 2021. https://www.niaaa.nih.gov

11. National Institute on Alcohol Abuse and Alcoholism (NIAAA). "Understanding Alcohol Use Disorder." *National Institute on Alcohol Abuse and Alcoholism*, U.S. Department of Health and Human Services, 2021. https://www.niaaa.nih.gov/publications/brochures-and-fact-sheets/understanding-alcohol-use-disorder

12. National Domestic Violence Hotline. *What Is Gaslighting?* thehotline.org, 2021. https://www.thehotline.org/resources/what-is-gaslighting

13. National Institute on Alcohol Abuse and Alcoholism (NIAAA). "Alcohol and Violence." *niaaa.nih.gov*, U.S.

Department of Health and Human Services. https://www.
niaaa.nih.gov/publications/alcohol-and-violence

14. American Psychological Association. "Alcohol Use and
Domestic Violence." *apa.org*, American Psychological
Association. https://www.apa.org/news/press/releases/
2014/03/alcohol-violence

15. Norström, Thor, and Hilde Pape. "Alcohol and
Divorce: Evidence from Norwegian Registry Data."
Addiction, vol. 105, no. 3, 2010, pp. 536–540. https://doi.
org/10.1111/j.1360-0443.2009.02802.x

16. U.S. Department of Health and Human Services. *Facing
Addiction in America: The Surgeon General's Report on
Alcohol, Drugs, and Health*. Chapter 2: The Neurobiology
of Substance Use, Misuse, and Addiction. 2016. https://
addiction.surgeongeneral.gov/sites/default/files/
surgeon-generals-report.pdf

17. Substance Abuse and Mental Health Services
Administration (SAMHSA). *Substance Abuse Treatment
and Domestic Violence*. Treatment Improvement Protocol
(TIP) Series 25. DHHS Publication No. (SMA) 12-4071.
Rockville, MD: U.S. Department of Health and Human
Services, 1997. https://www.ncbi.nlm.nih.gov/books/
NBK64330/

18. Meyers, R. J., Smith, J. E., & Lash, D. N. (2005). *A Program
for Engaging and Helping Substance-Abusing Individuals
Enter Treatment: The Community Reinforcement and Family
Training (CRAFT) Approach*. Journal of Rational-Emotive
and Cognitive-Behavior Therapy, 23(2), 153–166. https://
doi.org/10.1007/s10942-005-0018-2

19. Miller, W. R., Meyers, R. J., & Tonigan, J. S. (1999). Engaging
the unmotivated in treatment for alcohol problems: A
comparison of three strategies for intervention through

family members. *Psychology of Addictive Behaviors, 13*(4), 267–276. https://doi.org/10.1037/0893-164X.13.4.267

20. Kirby, K. C., & Baldwin, S. A. (2008). Community Reinforcement and Family Training (CRAFT): A comprehensive behavioral approach to help families of substance abusers. In A. M. Rowe & L. M. Liddle (Eds.), *Adolescent Substance Abuse: Research and Clinical Advances* (pp. 247–272). Cambridge University Press.

21. Lappan, S. N., Brown, J. J., & Barry, D. T. (2020). Dropout rates of in-person psychosocial substance use disorder treatments: A meta-analysis. *Addiction, 115*(7), 1135–1145. https://doi.org/10.1111/add.14997